I0113579

Cyprianus

Cyprianus:
St. Cyprian and the Black Book in Scandinavian Folklore
Copyright © 2025 Simone Kotva
All Rights Reserved.

ISBN 978-1-915933-73-7 (Hardcover)
ISBN 978-1-915933-74-4 (Softcover)

A CIP catalogue for this title is available from the British Library.
10 9 8 7 6 5 4 3 2 1

Except in the case of quotations embedded in critical articles or reviews,
no part of this book may be reproduced or transmitted in any form or by
any means, electronic or mechanical, including photocopying, recording,
or by any information storage and retrieval system, without permission in
writing from the publisher.

No part of this book may be used or reproduced in any manner for the
purpose of training artificial intelligence technologies or systems.

Simone Kotva has asserted her moral right to
be identified as the author of this work.

EU authorised representative:
Easy Access System Europe
Mustamäe tee 50, 10621 Tallinn, Estonia
gpsr.requests@easproject.com

Published in 2025
Hadean Press
West Yorkshire
England
https://hadean.press

Cyprianus

St. Cyprian and the Black Book in Scandinavian Folklore

Collected by Evald Tang Kristensen
Selected and translated by Simone Kotva

For Carl, Erik and Hayley

Contents

Introduction

Cyprianus is the name of an infamous grimoire in Scandinavian folk magic and a byword for sorcery. In recent years, dozens of *Cyprianus* books have been translated into English, revealing a rich array of folk-magical operations similar to those found in the Iberian Cyprian tradition. Missing from this emergent literature, however, is the place of folklore. The present volume provides a translation of Danish legends relating to the *Cyprianus,* originally collected in the second half of the nineteenth century by the folklorist Evald Tang Kristensen. Most of these legends refer to the *Cyprianus* as a book − its powers, familiar spirits and those persons bold (and sometimes foolish) enough to read from its pages − while others recount the exploits of its eponymous author, a mysterious figure who, in Scandinavian lore, takes on different guises and genders. Together, the legends offer a perspective on the *Cyprianus* that helps contemporary readers understand the cultural and folk-magical context of this fabled grimoire.

The *Cyprianus* in Scandinavian Folklore

Cyprianus books began appearing in Scandinavia during the mid-seventeenth century and all were originally copied by hand; printed books only date from the late eighteenth century onward. No two *Cyprianus* books are alike: with a few exceptions, the typical *Cyprianus* is a personalized collection of spells, rather than a manual of evocation.[1] However, Cyprian of Antioch is the eponym of the Scandinavian *Cyprianus*, and a significant number of books contains conjurations invoking the name of the Sorcerer Saint. These conjurations are all variants of the exorcistic *Prayer of St. Cyprian*, originally a medieval amuletic formula.[2] The practice of copying the Cyprianic *Prayer* into a small book and supplementing it with sundry workings and folk magical operations seems to have arrived to Scandinavia from the continent. Grimoires similar to the *Cyprianus* are familiar from the Iberian Peninsula, and it seems that the *Cyprianus* is a distant cousin of the Iberian Cyprian books. Aside

---

1 The exception to this rule is the Scandinavian practice of ascribing the authorship of Faust grimoires to Cyprian. See for instance the Faust grimoire held at the University of Lund manuscript collection, Manuscript no. 95654: https://www.alvin-portal.org/alvin/view.jsf?pid=alvin-record%3A95654&dswid=-9686 (accessed 20.09.2024). This practice is thought to derive from Germany, where Faust and Cyprian were sometimes confused, see Theodor von Zahn, *Cyprian von Antiochien und die deutsche Faustsage* (Erlangen, 1892).

2 Ferdinand Ohrt, "Cyprianus: Hans Bog og hans Bøn," *Danske studier* (1923): 1-21.

from sharing the *Prayer* with Iberian Cyprian books, Scandinavian *Cyprianus* books also have many spells in common with Iberian grimoires, and both types of compilations rose to popularity at roughly the same time during the early modern period.[3]

Also like their Iberian parallels (to which we will return shortly), Scandinavian Cyprian books quickly acquired a reputation that far outstripped their written content. In nineteenth-century Scandinavian culture, to mention the *Cyprianus* was to talk about something more than a grimoire. Indeed, ownership of an actual *Cyprianus* was a rare thing, not least because literacy was low and the printing of grimoires was outlawed until the end of the eighteenth century.[4] Instead, mention of the *Cyprianus* invoked into a conversation a host of fears, desires, dreams, and, of course, legends: fears of sorcery, desires for power, dreams of riches, and legends

---

3 Compare, for instance, the Iberian spells of the black cat and fava bean for invisibility, and their corresponding workings in Swedish Black Books. E.g. *The Book of St. Cyprian: The Sorcerer's Treasure*, trans. José *Leitão* (Hadean, 2014), 82-83, and Thomas Johnson, *Svartkonsböcker* (Revelore, 2019), 329, 424, 493. On Scandinavian Cyprian books, see Ane Ohrvik, *Medicine, Magic and Art in Early Modern Norway: Conceptualizing Knowledge* (Palgrave Macmillan, 2018), and Johannes Gårdbäck, "Cyprianus Förmaning" and "Cyprian Books of Magic in the Scandinavian Tradition," in *Cypriana: Old World*, eds. Alexander Cummins, Jesse Hathaway Diaz and Jenn Zahrt (Revelore, 2016), 36-82.

4 Kathleen Stokker, *Remedies and Rituals: Folk Medicine in Norway and the New Land* (Minnesota Historical Society Press, 2007), 75-105.

of wonder-working. Such legends provide vital – yet at times neglected – clues to appreciating the *Cyprianus* in its historical context.

In Scandinavian folklore, the *Cyprianus* is a book but also a character with its own designs and intentions. Today, we tend to think of objects as dead and inert and of books in particular as inanimate. It is what a person does with the book that matters, not what the book does on its own. A different view, according to which grimoires are, if not alive, then certainly enlivened, shapes much of the folkloric material relating to the *Cyprianus*. What does the *Cyprianus* do? Where does it come from? How does one interact with the *Cyprianus*? What risks are involved? These are some of the questions that recur in much of the Scandinavian folklore relating to the *Cyprianus*.

In this sense, Scandinavian folklore about Cyprian books has much in common with legends of the Iberian *Book of St. Cyprian*. Of the Iberian *Book of St. Cyprian*, José Leitão writes that it "has a certain kind of experience associated with it," and goes on to explain: "several actually."[5] These experiences are about sorcery, but also about society. They encompass "the highs and lows of fear and taboo, all of which frame the experience of *The Book of St. Cyprian* as a concept beyond the circumstantial words written in it."[6] Leitão distinguishes between two books, one printed (or, as was often the case, handwritten) and the other conceptual. It is this

---

5 José Leitão, *The Immaterial Book of St. Cyprian: Folk Concepts & Views on The Book as a Cultural Item Through the Reading of Folk Narratives* (Revelore, 2017), 12.

6 Leitão, *Immaterial Book*, 12.

"conceptual" book that Leitão identifies as folkloric or legendary. He even goes so far as to call the latter "immaterial," although this should not be interpreted as implying that the Cyprianic grimoires of folklore exist only in the imagination. Rather, Leitão's point is that a grimoire like the Iberian *Book of St. Cyprian* cannot be understood exhaustively by cataloguing its spells. In order to grasp the meaning of *The Book of St. Cyprian*, other cultural factors and, above all, cultural *experiences*, need to be taken into account. It is these experiences of a grimoire that coalesce in an "immaterial" book that is no less real for lacking a printed form.

Leitão, of course, is writing about Iberian Cyprian books that are different from Scandinavian *Cyprianus* grimoires. Most obvious among these differences is the religious context in which they were written. While the Iberian Peninsula was – and remains – predominantly Catholic, Scandinavia is Lutheran, and the Scandinavian Cyprian books all date from the post-Reformation period when Lutheran theology was enforced by law. The Lutheran context of Scandinavian Cyprian books has a noticeable influence on the folkloric material associated with grimoires. Significantly, the legendary author of the *Cyprianus* is no longer a saint and has lost his female co-martyr, St. Justina. Perhaps as a result of his spiritual status shifting, the contours of Cyprian's magic book also metamorphose. While the Iberian *Book of St. Cyprian* is associated with legends of treasure-hunting and disenchantment, the Scandinavian *Cyprianus* is identified with stories of the Devil and his master, the Black Book Priest or Black Book Minister.

Despite these differences, however, the two Cyprianic traditions – Iberian and Scandinavian – are related and go back to shared origins, as has already been mentioned. For this reason, my suggestion when reading the folklore translated here is to approach it as an example of what *Leitão* identifies as a grimoire's "framing experiences." The advantage of this approach is that it helps us to appreciate grimoire folklore as a tradition that stands in a dynamic and meaningful relationship to specific grimoires, without introducing a hierarchy between the two. Scandinavian Cyprian books contain a wealth of magical formulae, and the study of these formulae has been popular among scholars and practitioners alike, especially in recent years (I have myself written, on a previous occasion, about the contents of Norwegian *Cyprianus* books).[7] In the present volume, the reader is introduced to a different perspective on the Scandinavian Cyprianic tradition, one that complements the recent publication of Scandinavian Cyprian books in English translation by Thomas Johnson, Johannes Björn Gårdbäck and others.[8] This perspective takes root in legends about the *Cyprianus*, rather than in particular manuscripts, and has been influenced by the work of scholars such as Kathleen Stokker, who has situated the *Cyprianus* in the

---

7 Simone Kotva, *Cyprianic Conjurations from Norway* (Hadean, 2024).

8 Johnson, *Svartkonstböcker*; Gårdbäck, "Cypriaus Förmaning"; see also Johannes Björn Gårdbäck, *Trolldom: Spells and Methods of the Norse Folk Magic Tradition* (YIPPIE, 2015).

history of Scandinavian vernacular culture.[9] It is also indebted to the memory of those nineteenth-century folklorists without whom we would have little or no knowledge of Scandinavian sorcery and spirits.

Black Book, Priest and Devil:
Experiencing the *Cyprianus*

The legends translated in this book were first collected by the Danish folklorist Evald Tang Kristensen (1843-1929), in the latter half of the nineteenth century. By all accounts, Kristensen was a remarkable man: a school teacher by profession, he conducted the majority of his collecting during his free time, roaming the Danish countryside in search of disappearing rural customs and lore. Kristensen collected the full range of what in Danish is called *folkeminder,* "folk memories," from children's rhymes to agricultural practices and drinking songs. His collection is by far the most comprehensive in Danish, with Kristensen's published work amounting to over 12,000 pages, representing only half of the

---

9 Stokker, *Remedies and Rituals.* See also her articles, "To Catch a Thief: Binding and Loosing and the Black Book Minister," *Scandinavian Studies,* vol. 61, no. 4 (1989): 353–74; "Between Sin and Salvation: The Human Condition in Legends of the Black Book Minister," *Scandinavian Studies,* vol. 67, no. 1 (1995): 91–108; and "Narratives of Magic and Healing: 'Oldtidens Sortebog' in Norway and the New Land," *Scandinavian Studies,* vol. 73, no. 3 (2001): 399–416.

material gathered during his many journeys through rural Denmark.[10]

I have made selections from part 1 of the sixth volume of Kristenen's monumental *Danske Sagn som de har lydt i folkemunde* ("Danish Tales as Heard in Popular Lore"), subtitled *Djævelskunster, kloge mænd og koner* ("Devilish Arts, Cunning-Men and -Women"), first published in 1899. The material relating to the *Cyprianus* appears on pp. 59-130 and forms part of the section, "Om Fanden og forbund med ham," ("Of the Devil and pacts with him"). Kristensen preferred presenting the *Cyprianus* legends on their own, providing no context except for a note on provenance and an occasional name or initial. I have translated legends 70-80 and 175-131, omitting 208-213, which consist of Kristensen's personal collection of *Cyprianus* manuscripts. For readers interested in the contents of a typical *Cyprianus*, I suggest consulting Thomas Johnsen, *Svartkonstböcker* (Revelore, 2016). The manuscripts collected by Kristensen were subsequently analyzed by Ferdinand Ohrt, *Danmarks trylleformler*, 2 Vols (Copenhagen and Oslo, 1917-1921).

Kristensen's collection represents only a single region in Scandinavia, yet its portrayal of the *Cyprianus* is part of a broader, transnational tradition of folklore. Between 1380-1814 Norway was under Danish rule, while parts of what is now southern Sweden were only ceded from Denmark in 1720. Many of the stories collected by Kristensen refer to locations in what is now Norway and Sweden, and many of these stories are also

---

10 W. A. Craigie, "Evald Tang Kristensen, a Danish Folk-Lorist," *Folklore*, Vol. 9, No. 3 (1898): 194-225.

found in geographical locations far from Denmark.[11] Following Leitão, I suggest we read this folklore in terms of a set of cultural experiences framing the *Cyprianus*. Three such experiences or groups of experiences stand out as particularly prominent in the material collected by Kristensen: the qualities of the book itself, held-in-the-hand; encountering its owner, a person in possession of cunning, often a priest; and, most notorious of all, summoning the Devil by means of a *Cyprianus*. Woven through all these framing experiences are a number of origin stories, introducing the adventures of the book's eponymous author.

Black Book

The *Cyprianus* remembered by Kristensen's informants is often described as having a distinct appearance, a certain feel. According to the stories collected in *Danske Sagn*, a *Cyprianus* typically was black (although in one narrative it is red), written in alternating red and black ink. A common name for the *Cyprianus* in Danish was,

---

11 See Stokker, *Remedies and Rituals*, which traces the journey of the *Cyprianus* to North America via Norwegian immigrant communities. Southern Sweden is home to a striking collection of tales relating to the *Cyprianus*, for which see Gunnar Hyltén Cavallius, *Wärend och Wirdarne: Ett Försök i Svensk Etnologi*, Vol. 1(Stockholm, 1863), 327. According to Cavallius, the *Cyprianus* achieved legendary status as the "small" Black Book, contrasted to its "large" sister, typically a manual of evocation such as the enormously popular *Three-Fold Coercion of Hell of Dr. Johann Faustus*.

indeed, Black Book (*Sortebog*), an allusion to the color of its binding as well as to the Devil, whose powers are always connected to the color black in Scandinavian folklore. A *Cyprianus* was said to have two parts, one section devoted to summoning the Devil, the other to banishing him; one devoted to evil, the other to good. The morally ambiguous nature of the book is emphasized in Kristensen's collection. Like the Devil (more on him shortly), the *Cyprianus* serves those able to command it successfully, regardless of the conjuror's intent or morals.

Many stories collected by Kristensen dwell on the experience of opening this legendary book and reading it. A recurrent theme is the book's magnetism. Those who find the book are unable to put it down and are held in thrall by an enticing inscription at the bottom of each page compelling them to read on. Another theme is the book having a will of its own. The *Cyprianus* of folklore is difficult – sometimes impossible – to get rid of, evading ordinary attempts at destruction and rematerializing mysteriously, much to its owner's despair. Becoming master of the *Cyprianus* is also an ordeal. Legends 50 and 63 tell of a kind of initiation ritual, where mastery over the *Cyprianus* could only be gained by sleeping with the book pressed against one's bare skin, for three consecutive Thursday nights. (Performing a ritual on consecutive Thursday nights in order to become cunning or *klog* is a common theme in Scandinavian folklore and magic; here it is applied to the *Cyprianus.*) In all these stories the *Cyprianus* is an object of repulsion – but also of desire.

Cunning Folk and Black Book Priests

The second group of experiences framing the folkloric *Cyprianus* are encounters with the book's owners or better, masters and mistresses (for it is possible, in these stories, to own a copy of the *Cyprianus* without knowing how to use it properly). Those able to work the *Cyprianus* come in two types: *kloge folk*, or cunning-folk, on the one hand, and priests on the other. Scandinavian *kloge folk* were men and women suspected of sorcerous skill and special know-how, literally "wise people," "clever folk." Those mentioned in Cyprianic folklore are often characters whom people feared to cross; others are village healers known for their ability to charm and "bless" (*signe*). Alongside *kloge folk* one finds priests. A priest too might be described as *klog*, "wise" or "cunning," yet also possessed additional qualities. A common trope in Scandinavian folklore is the story – closely related to our *Cyprianus* legends, and also included in this translation – of the Devil's Black School (*Sorte skole)*. Every pastor was supposed to have attended this school, which involved making a pact with the Devil and then evading his power with cunning. Some Lutheran pastors became especially famed for their reputed command over the Devil, earning them the name of Black Book Priests (Norwegian, *svarteboksprester)*. Legends of priests acquiring the *Cyprianus* were often connected to their time studying theology in Germany, during which Scandinavian priests were thought to have attended the Devil's Black School. By the nineteenth century, it was widely believed by laypersons in Denmark and

Norway that every Lutheran priest had a *Cyprianus* in his possession.

In the legends relating to the *Cyprianus*, we find several stories featuring priests. One such story is the tale of a local vicar who, while preaching his Sunday sermon, senses that his *Cyprianus* is being tampered with and promptly returns home to discover someone – typically a terrified chambermaid – reading from the book. The vicar restores order by reciting a counter-formula from the book, banishing the unruly powers about to wreak havoc on his parish. Another recurrent motif is the vicar who exorcises by means of the *Cyprianus*, restoring health to those who have run afoul of spirits and sorcery. Although exorcism was strongly prohibited in Scandinavian Lutheranism, it remained a vital part of folk religiosity for several centuries after the Reformation, as these stories attest.[12]

Whether or not Lutheran priests were in fact regular users of the *Cyprianus* is impossible to say and ultimately a moot question. The significance of Black Book Priests in Scandinavian folklore lies less in their historicity and rather in what their ideas tell us about the practice of magic associated with the *Cyprianus*. The priest in Lutheran society was seen as a deeply pious figure – yet, through his assumed mastery over the *Cyprianus*, he was also understood to dance with the Devil. The close connection between the *Cyprianus* and priesthood in Kristensen's collection suggests that magic and religion cannot easily be separated in this type of conjuring: to

---

12 Linda Oja, *Varken Gud eller natur: synen på magi i 1600- och 1700-talets Sverige* (Stockholm, 1999).

work the *Cyprianus* was to have some insight into the activities of a priest, whether those activities were real or imagined.

The Devil and Animal Familiars

The Devil and his appearance is the third kind of experience framing the *Cyprianus*. In Kristensen's collection, those who recite from the *Cyprianus* may – wittingly or unwittingly – summon the Devil. The Devil often appears in human form, addressing the conjurer and demanding a reason for his summoning. If the conjurer is quick to reply, a pact is established, often to the conjurer's benefit. The Devil in human form can be bargained with and outwitted, granting boons to the person who is able to master the *Cyprianus*. Sometimes, however, the Devil outwits the conjurer. In Cyprianic folklore, an ill-formed pact with the Devil leads to ruin, madness and a tragic demise.

The Devil in Scandinavian folklore is more reminiscent of a demon in the Western grimoire tradition than he is of the Biblical Satan. In particular, the Devil in Kristensen's collection of *Cyprianus* legends acts very much like the first spirit who appears to Faust in the colorful preface of *The Three-Fold Coercion of Hell*.[13] The Devil also shares characteristics with the Scandinavian spirits known as trolls. Indeed, in one story – legend 70 –

---

13 *Magia Naturalis et Innaturalis: or, Threefold Coercion of Hell, Last Testament and the Sigils of the Art*, trans. Nicolás Álvarez (Enodia, 2019).

the Black Book Priest tells the young boy who has just been apprehended reading the *Cyprianus* (and unwittingly conjured a mass of serpents), "that he should thank God that he [i.e. the priest] had arrived so quickly, for if the snakes had disappeared, the troll himself would have come, and there would have been no help for him." Trolls in Scandinavian folklore come in a variety of forms, from the beautiful to the hideous, but they are typically untrustworthy and will grant boons only to the quick-witted. The most common word for sorcery in Kristensen's collection of *Cyprianus* legends is, indeed, *trolddom*, a word whose literal meaning is "domain of trolls" and suggests a person's facility negotiating with spirits and the enchantments cast by spirits.

A human form is only one of many appearances taken by the Devil in Kristensen's collection, however. Reading from the *Cyprianus* also conjures dwarves, red imps and, even, in one place, a glowing wheel. Animal forms are the most common. When someone who lacks cunning reads from the *Cyprianus*, animals may appear suddenly and behave in unsettling ways. In some legends, the animals are identified as the Devil in bestial form, especially when the animal in question is a black dog. In others, the demonic identity is implicit. A great variety of animals are listed in the stories. Aside from dogs, we find cats, owls, canaries, geese, hares, bulls, flies, rams, crows, ravens, snakes, toads, hens and black roosters. In Scandinavian folklore, Odin is associated with black dogs and corvids, and Odin himself is described as a man dressed in black. These overlaps between the *Cyprianus* and folklore associated with Oden may be coincidental, but it is more likely that they are the result of a protracted period of cultural encounter and exchange, during which continental material has combined with local traditions.

The Scandinavian Cyprian

Finally, the experiences framing the *Cyprianus* echo with rumors of its eponymous author. Shorn of sainthood, the post-Reformation Cyprian of Scandinavian Black Books becomes part of a Protestant context. Only in one of the stories translated here – legend 21– do we find a story reminiscent of the original hagiography of St. Cyprian of Antioch. Here, Cyprian is a Bishop who devotes half his life to evil and the other half to good. In the majority of the Scandinavian origin stories, however, Cyprian takes on new identities. Kathleen Stokker, who has studied the *Cyprianus* in its cultural context, describes local customs of portraying Cyprian "as a Dane too evil even for Hell, from which he was expelled…Disgusted by his expulsion, Cyprianus returned home, it was said, and wrote nine books full of [magical arts], the basis of all the subsequently circulating Black Books."[14] In Kristensen's collection, Cyprian is somewhat less sinister. One recurring portrait of Cyprian is as the companion of Henrik Smid. Smid (or Smed, Smith, Smidt; the spelling varies) was a Danish physician who lived during the sixteenth century in what is now southern Sweden.

---

14 Stokker, "Narratives of Magic and Healing," 406, discussing the work of Aasbjørn Sæbø.

Smid was the author of several popular books on medical science, including the hugely influential *Hinrick Smids Lægebog* ("Henrik Smid's Book of Cures"), first published in 1599. *Hinrick Smids Lægebog* was a household item in much of southern Scandinavia well into the nineteenth century and is mentioned in a number of Kristensen's stories translated here. Cyprian himself is described as Smid's friend or brother, and the two figures – and their respective books – appear to form a close relationship. One reason for this close relationship may be found in the date of Smid's text: *Hinrick Smids Lægebog* was published at roughly the same time as the Cyprianic tradition reached Scandinavia from the continent. However, the overlap in content between Black Books and medical books such as Smid's volume is also significant.[15] Many Cyprian books in Scandinavia are weighted toward the treatment of disease and contain a mixture of medical as well as sorcerous cures. Added to this, the lengthy Cyprianic conjurations in Black Books show Cyprian as an exorcist able to heal illness through divine power. The connection between Cyprian and Henrik Smid throws light on the role of Cyprian as *healer*, an important but sometimes overlooked aspect of his tradition in Scandinavia.

Also overlooked in Cyprian's Scandinavian tradition is his connection to female figures. The Cyprian of the Scandinavian *Cyprianus* has lost his female co-martyr, St. Justina. Yet, in Kristensen's collection, authorship of the *Cyprianus* is popularly ascribed to women. In part, this is

---

15 Anna-Elisabeth Brade, "Efterskrift," in *Henrik Smiths Lægebog I-VI* (Copenhagen, 1976), 20.

due to *Oldtidens Sortebog* ("The Black Book of Yore"), a printed *Cyprianus* from the latter half of the nineteenth century. In this "gory gothic tale" set in the fourteenth century, Cyprian is not a priest but a ravishingly beautiful Mexican *nun* abducted by lascivious monks.[16] While imprisoned by the monks, Cyprian writes her book of magic, mixing the ink from her own blood. An oral version of the preface of *Oldtidens Sortebog* appears in Kristensen's collection (legend 20) where we find Cyprian writing her book "with the blood of her heart and with will-o'-the-wisp *(hjærteblod og lysebrand)*." Kristensen collected two additional origin stories in which women play an important role. One is the short but evocative legend 19 in which we learn that the original *Cyprianus* was written by seven condemned sorceresses. Before being led to the stake, the seven witches were commanded to commit their magic to paper and thus composed the first *Cyprianus*. In another story, legend 17, Cyprian is "Cypri," one of the first Christians. His wife, Ane, is a pagan and a witch, "cunning in all dark arts." After years spent undoing and countering Ane's sorcery, Cypri becomes even more skilled than his wife and eventually commits his knowledge to posterity in the form of the first *Cyprianus*.

---

16 Stokker, "Narratives of Magic and Healing," 406.

Legends of the Cyprianus in translation

Note on the Text and Translation

When arranging Kristensen's narratives, I have followed Kristensen's sequence within each section, but have provided new numbering to avoid undue confusion, since my translation is a selection. For those wishing to consult *Danske Sagn*, Kristensen's original numbering is provided in the Appendix. I have followed Kristensen's headings for the sections, but have expanded some headings slightly to reflect the contents of the legends.

I have attempted to reflect the colloquial quality of Kristensen's recorded narratives as best as possible, although the full nuances of these long-lost voices cannot be conveyed adequately in translation. When translating words relating to magic, I have taken a decision to adopt the following conventions that are observed throughout the text: 1) "cunning," "cunning-man," "cunning-woman," "cunning folk" reflect *klog/ klogskap, klog mand, klog kone, kloge folk*, concepts centered around sorcerous know-how as well as general wisdom and cleverness; 2) "sorcery," "sorcerous arts," "sorcerer," "sorceress" translates *trolddom, trolddomskunster, troldmand, troldkvinde*, words that indicates dealings with trolls, their enchantments and enchantments in general; 3) while "witchcraft," "witch" and "witchdoctor" translates *heksekunst*, *heks* and *heksemester*, words synonymous with *trolddom* but with more limited popularity as ways of describing sorcery.

Many stories in Kristensen's collection describe people "reading" from the Cyprianus and "reading" is often a shorthand for magic. In Danish (as in Swedish and Norwegian), "reading" (*læsing*), when associated with folk magic, does not mean silent reading. Rather, it means the recitation of a verbal charm either memorized or printed; it can also indicate the recitation of a conjuration that will summon a spirit. In the latter context, "to read back" (*læse tilbage*) means to banish a spirit, sending it back to its place of origin. Since "to read" is a key expression in Scandinavian folk magic, I have often opted for a literal translation, indicating the meaning of the expression in square brackets.

1. The Black School

1. Three arrive to the Black School at a time, and one must belong to the Devil if he does not fulfil a promise made to him [i.e. the Devil]; for example, never to tie or wear more than one garter. In Ris, some years ago, there was a priest who had attended the Black School. *Nis Callesen.*

❉

2. Those who attend the Black School must all make a promise to do something for the rest of their lives. For instance, Pastor Petersen in Ris always used only one glove, and Pastor Mygind in Stepping never had his chafing dish cleaned.
Nis C.

❉

3. All priests must attend the Black School. Once, the Devil seized the shadow of one, so he had none when the sun shone on the field. The Devil wanted to grab the person, since he was last [to leave the school], but only caught his shadow.
Kristen Ebbesen, Egtved

❉

4. The priests who attended the Black School must perform a specific task at certain times throughout their lives. A priest in Hojrup walked two miles every day, and in bad weather, he paced the miles at home on his living room floor. A priest in Ringe never wore gloves, no matter how cold it was, he never did. Of a priest on Ærø, it was said that every time he entered the church, he stopped in the vestibule, unbuttoned all the buttons on his clerical robe, and buttoned it up again before going inside.

Sødinge school

Ж

5. Once there were eleven priests who had graduated from the Black School, but it was vital for them all to escape, since the teacher [of the Black School] always keeps the last one. However, one of them, a cunning-woman's son, found a solution. All eleven grasped each other's hands and formed a circle and began dancing as if possessed, spinning out of the wide gates of Hell so that no one was left behind, and they all escaped unharmed.

A.L.

Ж

6. Those who attend the Black School run out when they are finished because the one who is last to leave belongs to the Devil. Once, a priest was the last to leave, but he was clever enough to tell the Devil he must seize his shadow first, and with that, the Devil was satisfied. Afterward, the priest had no shadow, and

the Devil often wore it, going around with it, so people believed they saw the priest in the fields and other places, even though he was at home in his house.
P.K. Madsen

※

7. Many stories are told about the Black School which priests used to attend in the old days to learn how to summon ghosts and other such creatures. In return for learning these things, it was promised to the Devil that he would have the last person to leave the school once they were finished. That was the worst part of it all, for most of them were willing to go through the training, and it was indeed needed at a time when such disturbances were common. Once, a group had completed their exams and was about to leave the school when the Devil was immediately ready to seize the last one. But one of them wasn't easily fooled and said, calmly, "Wait a moment while I tie my garter." From that day on, the man never wore a garter, and thus the Devil was tricked that time.
Søren Hansen

※

8. The old priest in Bedding, Rosendal, who was there before Broch, had attended the Black School. For this reason, he could perform certain feats. But since he was the last one to leave the school, he was supposed to belong to the Devil. So, he made a deal in order to be free: he would never get out of bed and dress unless there was a light on the table. He came here from the heath and preached in both a German and a Danish church. But once, the vicarage caught fire, and he nearly burned to death. Finally, his wife remembered him and ran in to place a lit candle on the table for him. Only then did he get up. It is also known that when he lay down, he slept in his clothes and boots and often on chairs.

Pr. M.

※

9. The priest Henne in Mørhe was never allowed to have half of his beard shaved off. It was a pact he had made with the Devil, and as long as he didn't break it, the Devil had no power over him.

Søren Nielsen, Carpenter, Søby

※

10. Money-Lavst had made a pact with the Devil, and after a certain number of years, he had to come and take him. And sure enough, the Devil arrived on time. The priest asked if he could go up to the church and say a prayer first. Yes, the Devil allowed it, and the priest went. The Devil dared not enter the church, but when it took a while, he finally shouted into [the building], asking if the priest wasn't coming soon. The priest replied, "Yes, but could you give me time while I tie my left garter?" The Devil agreed. But the priest

never tied it, and thus the Devil could not take him.
Peder Jensen Pedersen, Thomaskjær

⚡

11. A person told me some time ago that in Kragelund parish, there once lived a very clever dean who had attended the Black School. My informant didn't know where this Black School was located, but it was said that the Devil himself was head teacher there, and every year he had to take one of the students. They drew lots to see whom the Devil would take, and one year, the lot fell on Dean Kragelund. But he was a cunning and clever fellow, and when the Devil was about to take him away, he asked for a reprieve until he could tie his garter. The Devil granted it, and the dean happily stuffed the garter into his pocket. He never tied it.
Svend Peter Jensen

2. *Cyprianus*: The Book – Cyprian's Exploits – Henrik Smid

12. Every other page in a *Cyprianus* has red letters, and every other page has black ones.
J- M.

⚜

13. A *Cyprianus* has two sections, which are called Nebrianus and Debrianus.
Hadsund.

⚜

14. There were thirteen Books of Moses, and they were about the old Egyptian teachings.
E. T. K.

⚜

15. I used to own a *Cyprianus*. There were two sections in it that were outlined in triangles. In one you could read about how to summon the Devil, and in the other, how to send him away. When they wanted to perform the recitation, they were to turn the book around and read it upside down.
Peder Bærtelsen, Sørup.

⚜

16. He who wants to read a *Cyprianus* must have a loaf of rye bread lying by his side and a good stick, and then some linseed, to be scattered on the floor. When the Evil One arrives, and one becomes embarrassed with him, then one should either make him dissolve the seeds or break the bread into pieces, and since he can't do either, he is forced to leave again.
Kristen Frederiksen, North Bindslev.

𝕏

17. One of the first Christians, whose name was Cypri, had a wife, whose name was Ane, and she was a pagan and a truly wicked person, cunning in all dark arts. Her husband and others tried repeatedly to persuade her to become a Christian, but they were unsuccessful, and she practiced her arts whenever opportunity arose. Her husband repaired all the damage she caused, for he was even more adept at the art than she was, and he recorded all the arts she had practicd and those he had countered. After her death, he gave the book to a good friend of his who was a priest, so that he could benefit from it. He transcribed several books based on it and gave them to other priests, and in the old days, every priest owned that book; but I doubt they still do. You can only see it [i.e. the *Cyprianus*] in the large bookstalls in Copenhagen. Since it is written in Latin, only priests can use it properly, and that is why, if a layman gets hold of it, he will end up causing much harm, since he does not understand what he is reading.
I. Kr. Jensen.

Ж

18. It is said of the *Cyprianus* that, originally, it was written by Moses as a continuation of the five Books of Moses and thus should be a Sixth Book of Moses. It contained all the sorcerous arts of the Egyptians, and for this reason it should not be counted among the sacred scriptures.

P. Jensen.

Ж

19. There were seven sorceresses who were about to be burned. But before [they were burned] they were charged, in addition to their sentence, to write down how they had performed all their arts. So they wrote them down, all seven of them separately, and it was gathered into a book which was called the *Cyprianus*.

Ole Kristensen, Smidstrup.

Ж

20. A woman was supposed to have written the *Cyprianus*. She was taken to a monastery by some monks and for a long time she sat deep in the earth under the monastery so that nobody would know she was there. The men wanted to have their way with her, you see. That was where she wrote the *Cyprianus* with the blood of her heart and with will-o'-the-wisp (*hjærteblod og lysebrand*). From these two [ingredients] she mixed the ink, which, as you know, is red. The only person who came down to her was Father John, but she deceived him in the end so that he remained in the cave and she returned wearing his clothes because she had made him remove his clothes, you see. And then she escaped the monastery.

Egtved.

⚒

21. Niels Kristensen from Hald cured old Krabbe of an illness the doctors had given up on; for this reason, he received a pension from the farm. He is known in many regions where he has wandered about and healed the sick. He wanders about fields and collects plants there, and in the village pond he collects aquatic plants and then makes remedies from them. I once had a longer conversation with this man and I want to present, here, what he told me:

"The *Cyprianus* is written by a very learned bishop named Cyprianus. He spent half of his life experiencing all the good a person can experience, and the other half experiencing all the evil imaginable. All his learning and experience he recorded in the famous work, which consists of sixteen volumes. The first four deal with religion, and the next four deal with angels and devils. Then there are discussions of medicine and poisonous herbs, and finally about many hidden or not very familiar arts and experiments that can either benefit or harm one's fellow human beings. At that time and for a long time after, most people could neither read nor write, and this gave rise to the book's

dubious reputation. It was believed that the book could not be burned."
J. J., Refsh[aløen].

)(

22. There is a wicked book of sorcery called *The Black Moses.* A man who lives out in Spjarup thicket said he had read from it. This was with an old schoolmaster who stayed with him for a time and lived off his pension. Later, the schoolmaster travelled to the Haderslev area and took the book with him. The man said it was unpleasant to read.
Kristen Ebbesen, Egtved.

)(

23. Steffen Tømrer from Rodstrup had an old Bible which contained *The Sixth Book of Moses.* When he wanted to read a psalm from it, he could make a person go mad instantly. He could also reveal thieves, etc.
According to Hans Hansen, Jakob Rasmussen, Stensby.

)(

24. Belief in the *Cyprianus* still exists, but this precious book is only in the possession of a few. Eske Olesen from Ås was believed to have had it several years ago. It is said that when pastor Jordhoj came to visit him, the priest exclaimed, "Are you here, you unclean spirit, then go away!" – "No, go away, I have nothing to do with the evil spirit."

Last year, one Søren Andersen from Toftum claimed to possess it [i.e. the *Cyprianus*] and was so precise with it that he was able to inform a man that not only had five – but forty – *riksdaler* been stolen from him! He also identified the thief but accused the wrong person, was summoned before the Conciliation Commission, and had to make amends.

H. Br.

X

25. One day when I worked in Engesvang I was supposed to visit my wife's mother, who was called Forest-Ane, and collect a book. I was told not to look in it, but I dared to do so anyway, and at the bottom of each page was written in large red letters: "Turn over the page, turn over the page!" Then I could well sense that something was not right with that book. It must have been a *Cyprianus*.

J. J., Refsh[aløen].

X

26. Down here in Smidstrup, there is a man who has read too widely, and there was such music inside his walls, they could hear it sometimes in one place and sometimes in another. Jens Kuske's son-in-law, whose name is Thomas Skytte, inherited a *Cyprianus* from him, and his second wife inherited the cunning from her husband, so they now turned to her in that matter.

She also stashed it away in a public bench in Smidstrup town, right next to the pavement.
Karen Frederiksdatter.

)(

27. They asked someone if he had a *Cyprianus*. He said yes, and of course they wanted to see it before they believed. Another person was then given it so he could read a bit, and he thought he would hold onto it, so they wouldn't get it from him at first; he wanted to have read something in it. But the owner grabs it, and it disappears from his hand, even though he clutched it tightly.
Egtved.

)(

28. Stiff-Kræn owned a *Cyprianus*. He had acquired it down in Torslev from a man who had four [copies], but he never used it. One time, however, he had taken it down from the shelf and sat reading in it. Just as he was sitting there a whetstone, which was standing right next to him, split in two and it made a noise as if someone could have fired a gun right next to him. Now he became frightened and returned the *Cyprianus* to its shelf. I was supposed to have it from him, and we had agreed on a day when he was supposed to bring it. But then my father made me run an errand in town, and he also told me what was written on the title page of it. When I heard that, I'd had enough. Stiff-Kræn did come, and since I wasn't home, he went to Lørslev, and

I didn't acquire any book.
Jens Peder Pedersen, Ilbjærge.

※

29. There was one person here who acquired a
Cyprianus from a sack of rags in Åby.
Kristen Nielsen, Mosehuse.

※

30. They also had a *Cyprianus* at Overgård; it lay open
on a small ledge in "the yellow silk room." People who
served there around fifty years ago or so have seen it.
Karen Marie Rasmussen.

※

31. The parish clerk's daughter in Gjødvad served in
the vicarage alongside Priest-Jens. They were good
friends, and he persuaded her to steal a *Cyprianus* from
the priest, and this was how he acquired his knowledge.
Gjødvad.

※

32. A man has lived here in Glenstrup village. He had
a *Cyprianus* and cured according to it.
Niels Jensen, Glenstrup.

※

33. When one employs a *Henrik Smid* in conjunction with a *Cyprianus,* one can perform almost any witchcraft one desires.

J. M.

𝕏

34. Henrik Smid was one of Cyprian's brothers. He was a skilled physician, and there was a queen in labor, but she didn't want any man to deliver her child. So, he put on women's clothing and entered and delivered her. But they became suspicious when they ate at the feast. They didn't want to let him examine, but he was to be tricked in a way that they let a golden apple roll around on the table to each of them and into their lap. Women usually spread their knees apart when they take hold of something like that, but he closed his knees, and then he was discovered. He was to be punished, for the queen had so sternly forbidden men to come to her, and so his tongue was cut out of his throat. That was when he started writing the medical book.

Lars Nielsen, Vinkel.

𝕏

35. Regarding the well-known, diligent writer Henrik Smid in Malmö, I heard the following story in Nordfyn: He was a brother of Cyprianus, and both were very learned and wise men; however, the latter used his knowledge in the service of evil, while the former was a good man who had written several medical books, which also contained witchcraft, just like the book, *Cyprianus*, but only with good intentions. Henrik Smid met a sorrowful end. Once, the Swedish queen was in labor, and no one could deliver her, even though they summoned all the most skilled midwives. It was forbidden for any man to assist the queen; however, Smid, who was an experienced physician, disguised himself as a woman and successfully delivered the queen. There was great joy, and much praise was given to the fortunate midwife. But, to his misfortune, it was discovered that he was a man, for which he had to endure harsh imprisonment and was shackled and placed in iron collars. However, every time they tightened them [the collars], they sprang open again; but in the end, Henrik Smid was beheaded.

Anton Andersen.

☿

36. There is a good book that contains many good things, and that is the *Henrik Smid*. A man whom I worked for had that book, but we were not allowed to see it. Nevertheless, we sneaked a look at it when he wasn't home. The *Cyprianus* is said to be even better. There were three brothers who studied these matters, and each made a book, namely Henrik Smid, Cyprianus, and Hans Mikkelsen.[17]

Tåning

☿

---

17 Hans Mikkelsen, Bishop of Odense 1626-1641.

37. Many years ago, when I was working for the hunting squire in Stenderup forest, we had a kitchen maid whose grandmother was from Gudsø. This grandmother was called a witch. The maid told me that her grandmother had the book, *Cyprianus*. So I said to her, "When you visit there sometime, couldn't you borrow it from her? I would really like to see that book." – "Yes," she said, "but I don't think it will help; she probably won't lend it. But I'll try to get hold of it when I visit, and it won't be long before that happens." And she did get it for me. But she didn't ask for it; she just took it. "Because I knew," she said, "that when grandmother missed her book, she would soon get it back."

It was written in red and black and was only an excerpt from the larger book she had. It was striking to see that whenever it described performing magic, such as becoming invisible, revealing thieves, calming panicked horses, staunching blood, giving advice for bewitched animals, or anything else, it was done by taking the Lord's name in vain. It said in the book, "Revealing thieves is no art; becoming invisible for twenty-four hours is no art." And likewise with blessings, it was done by calling on the Devil and also by taking the Lord's name in vain. But when it came to conjuring (*mane*), it said, "This is done simply by faith in the Lord's name in conjunction with the sign of the cross," for that was to oppose evil, and for that, there was no need to call on him [i.e. the Devil]. But it was to drive away evil, not summon it. It is my belief that this has been confirmed to me several times. "But it is indeed an art to take four bushels of grain from a load of rye when it is to be brought into the house, to take four bushels from it in each part of the field the load passes through." That was an art, it said. This also happened by calling on the Devil.

When the maid left the hunting squire, I forgot to give her the book back. It was always kept under lock and key in my chest, yet it suddenly disappeared. It probably happened just as the maid said: when her grandmother missed the book, she would find a way to retrieve it. The book stated everywhere that in order to perform any art, the Devil's name had to be mentioned so many times, followed by the Lord's name. But the only place in the book where it didn't say the Devil's name had to be mentioned was in conjuring (*mane*); this was done solely through faith in the name of the Triune God and by the sign of the cross. This has strengthened my belief that to drive away evil, nothing more is needed than faith in the name of the Triune God.
Hans Jokum Lauritsen, Vejen.

⚶

38. I don't believe in ghosts or supernatural things; such things don't exist these days. It's just as well that people are not so cunning anymore, because people used to harm each other that way. In the past, they could do these things, I know that well enough; back then, there were seven books of Moses in the Bible, but two were removed because people were becoming too cunning. Those two books contained a lot of information about all sorts of things people could learn.

Over in Fjelde on Lolland, there was a man who had the authentic *Cyprianus*, and he was also very skilled. When he was at a harvest feast or some other gathering, and a roast chicken, duck, or goose was brought to the table, if the cunning-man was in the mood, he could make the roast fowl stand up and flap its wings. See, he knew more than his Lord's Prayer. There was a time when some people in the town couldn't make butter; so they went to the cunning-man and got something to put in the churn, and it was supposed to help. The one who had taken their butter-luck would likely come and try to borrow something from them, but they had to make sure she didn't get anything; otherwise, it wouldn't work. Sure enough, an old woman came around when it was time to churn and wanted to borrow a needle; they said, "no," and refused as best they could, but she was persistent and eventually acquired the needle. So, of course, it didn't work. In another place in town where they had the same problem, she came and wanted to borrow a strainer or a milking pail – whichever it was – and got it, no matter how much they resisted, and so it didn't work there either.

Told by a tavern keeper in Nykøbing, whose wife was born in Fjelde on Lolland.
Karen Toxværd.

39. When Marie Jyde was a child, they once had an
ill animal on the farm where she was raised, so they
sent for a wise woman who lived nearby. She came
and brought her *Cyprianus* with her; she put it aside
while she went into another room to be served. Now,
Marie and the son (a boy her age) noticed the book and
naturally became curious and decided to read it; but no
sooner had they opened it and started reading than the
woman came rushing in, gave each of them a slap over
the ear, and snatched the book from them. She said that
if they had read more of it, something bad would have
happened to them. Marie couldn't remember what they
had read – it was in red and black letters, large and
small mixed together – but they could definitely read it
well. She is now a woman of about fifty years.
From East Lolland, as told by Karen Toxværd in Sillestrup.

※

40. Old Majland had a *Cyprianus*; I have read it. It
began like this: "What harm did it do Moses to learn all
the Egyptian scientific arts when he only did good with
them? Go and do likewise." A couple of pages he had
glued together. "You must certainly not read those," he
told me. He was the toughest man, I believe, in all of
Northern Jutland, truly a giant. He had become angry
at the parish clerk, and one day he came to me and
asked if I hadn't noticed that the parish clerk was blind
in one eye. "Yes, I do think he sees poorly with it." –
"Then I'll make sure the other one goes blind too." He
then drew a circle with chalk on the seat of a chair and

jabbed a fork into it. "Now it [i.e. the eye] will soon be blind." His housekeeper was supposed to check on it [i.e. the situation], and she said that now both eyes were blind. He was happy about that because now Satan couldn't see and steal his cabbages. By then, Majland was so old that he couldn't go anywhere.

Rodding. I once visited Majland, but he was very suspicious of me, insulted me terribly, and finally became so coarse that I had to leave, telling his son-in-law, who disapproved of his behavior, that it wouldn't be out of order if I complained to the police. E. T. K.

X

41. Shortly before the pastor passed away, he got rid of his books, and it was very important to him, because whoever does not manage to sell them before he dies belongs to the Devil. The third person who ends up with them can never get rid of them; he certainly belongs to the Devil. The *Henrik Smid* and the *Cyprianus* went to farmer Jens Pedersen in Kildebrønde, the book of witchcraft went to old Sidse Jens Frederiks in Tune, and her husband is still alive. Jens Pedersen became a wretched man because he died, being the third person who had the books, and he could not get rid of them no matter how hard he tried. In his last years, he was confused and mad, and he could never find peace unless someone was sitting and playing for him. His death was also dreadful, as he was torn apart in his bed by the Devil. The books were placed under his head in his coffin.

Tune.

42. There was an old witch they called Ane Klit; she could transform herself into a hare. When she died, they needed to have her belongings inventoried, and they went through them to see if she had a *Cyprianus*. My father looked through the books, and then the priest, Mr. Højland, who was on the poor relief committee, asked, "What is he looking for?" – "Oh," he replied, "I was wondering if she had any fancy historical books." – "Yes, I know what he's looking for, but she doesn't have a *Cyprianus*, it's too expensive a book for her. It was translated from French by someone named Anus, and 'Cypri' means 'translated'." That's how the priest explained it to my father.
Niels Jensen, Hemmet.

43. The priest Mr. Gede was called to a smallholder named Thomas Klode who lived down by the Moselund hills to give him last rites. He was quite peculiar. As soon as the priest opened the door, he said to himself, "Well, so that's how it is here." He then went in and took a book with him. The servant who drove him saw this and said that it was a large book. Then he backed out of the door and drove home again. It wasn't long before the man died.
Sören Andersen, Engesvang.

44. Mr. Gede was the vicar here from 1859 to 1873. In a house in Mosehind lived Thomas Klode, who suffered from a peculiar illness. He couldn't work and would stand outside his house for half the day with his back against the door, staring over at the heathland. But it was a place where few people passed by. Eventually, he became bedridden. People said that he could not die because he had a *Cyprianus* in his house. So, a message was sent to the vicar, asking him to come and minister to him. The priest had also heard the talk about a *Cyprianus* and spoke with the man about it. Yes, he had the book, and the priest took it with him. He placed it under his cassock, when he was in his carriage, but when he crossed Tålund heath, they passed a waterhole, and an invisible hand came and snatched the book from the priest and threw it into the pond. But he was quick, jumped out, and retrieved the book, holding tightly onto it until he got home. There he placed it in his bookcase, but the next morning it was gone; someone had taken it during the night. He could guess where it was and went there to retrieve it. He got the book back and kept it in such a way that it wouldn't be lost again. A few days later, the man also died.

J. P. Abo, Engesvælg.

3. Disposing of a *Cyprianus*

45. A *Cyprianus* passes through three owners and follows the third owner to the grave.
Nik. Chr.

X

46. The *Cyprianus* cannot be burned.
H. V. R.

X

47. A *Cyprianus* cannot be burned in any other way than by leaving some ashes in the top of the oven when baking, and pushing them together, then placing the bread in and throwing it onto the ashes on top of the bread. Otherwise, it always flies out of the fire again.
E. T. K.

X

48. A cunning-woman can only get rid of her books by giving them to a man, and a cunning-man can only dispose of them by giving them to a woman.
M. Møller

X

49. One can get rid of a *Cyprianus* by taking it to a crossroads and relieving oneself on it at midnight. *Ribe region. E. T. K.*

X

50. A *Cyprianus* could only be acquired by sleeping with it on one's bare chest for three Thursday nights in a row. The tenth person who had it in their possession could not get rid of it; it could be burned and buried, but it would always come back. The nine others could have it and perform magic with it, and even get rid of it. But it was difficult to know who the tenth person was. *P. Nielsen (school teacher), Skuderløse.*

X

51. The daughter or granddaughter of the man who had inherited the book from her father wanted to get rid of it. She then attached it to a stone with an iron clamp, which was so heavy that only two men could carry it, and had the stone thrown into the sea (the water). But when she got home, it was back in its old place. The man who had owned the *Cyprianus* forced a thief, who had stolen thirty ells of canvas, to walk seven miles in his bare linens and return the stolen goods [i.e. in his underclothes]. On the way, he had to wade through a stream.
O. Chr. B.

※

52. The third person who acquired a *Cyprianus* could not get rid of it. There was a blacksmith in Regtrup near Klavsholm named Anders Lyng who had received it, but unfortunately, he became the third owner, and nothing he did to get rid of it helped. He had moved from another town called Matrup to Regtrup in an attempt to rid himself of his *Cyprianus*. After selling his house, he fastened the book to a piece of timber and left. But when he arrived in Regtrup, the book was on the table in his new residence. Seeing it again made him so frustrated that he went to the forge, set a fire, and threw the book into it, thinking it was completely burned to ashes. However, when he entered his living room, he found the book back on the table. From that time on, he was constantly unlucky.
Vrinders.

※

53. Old Peder Lang in Vinkel was something of a witchdoctor, and he also owned a *Cyprianus*. But he wanted to get rid of it. "I put that damn book in the stove so that it was completely burned up, but shortly after, it was back in my cupboard. So I took it down to Tapdrup Lake, tied a large stone to it, and put it under the ice, but when I came home, the damn book was back in my cupboard." He could manipulate the wind, he thought, and when he entered somewhere and the boys were making a racket, he would start talking harshly to them, saying, "You need to behave yourselves. If you don't behave, I can just as well swallow you as I can swallow that large stone outside." He lived in the same house as an old woman, and they shared the same front door. When he died, she knew that he couldn't get into Heaven because he had been a cunning-man, so she went into town, borrowed a straw stack, and placed it in front of the door. She knew that before the Devil could get in, he would have to break every straw in the stack.

Niels Simonsen, Vejrum.

X

54. Per Lang also tried to burn his *Cyprianus* in the oven, and he saw that it burned, but when he came in, it was still in his chest. Per Lang was a strange apparition; there was no one I was as afraid of as him. When he came, he would ask me if I had washed. "If you're not washed, I'll swallow you, and I can just as well swallow you as I can swallow the thorn bush that stands on Tromholt's dyke." I thought it was dreadful to hear.

Rasmus Nielsen, Vinkel.

X

55. A man inherited a *Cyprianus*, but he was tired of it and wanted to get rid of it. He tried to give the book away, but it kept coming back. He even buried it in the ground. One day, when they were baking, he thought that now he would finally be rid of it, so he sneaked in and threw the book into the oven. Now he thought he had finally gotten rid of it. But shortly after, he happened to feel his breast pocket, where he usually kept it, and the book was still there.

L. N. Bertelsen, Øster-Vandet.

※

56. Concerning the blacksmith's wife mentioned in *Skattegraveren*, Vol. 4, no. 557, an old woman in this town has said that she cured many and dealt with all sorts of things.[18] She possessed a *Cyprianus*, which was written in human blood, and whoever possessed it was in league with the Devil. The book had been passed down in the family, but the blacksmith's wife was tired of it and sought to get rid of it. Therefore, she tried several times to send it away, but it always came back to the house at night.

P. Hvidtfeldt, Kolding.

※

57. A man named Per Væver lived up here on the Vandtrang hills, and he met with such misfortune. He went to an auction and bought a lot of books, including a *Cyprianus*. He became curious and started reading it, and he attracted the Evil One to himself, but he couldn't get rid of him. The Evil One appeared

---

18 *Skattegraveren* ("The Treasure-Seeker") was a journal of folklore studies, edited by Evald Tang Kristensen.

every night and lay under their stove as a large black dog with a ringed tail. He tried to get rid of the book, but it was no use. He went out north of the house to the boundary between Restrup Mark and Sønderholm Mark and dug for water to throw the book in. He dug a hole sixty fathoms deep, working both day and night, but still couldn't reach the water. He went inside, grabbed the book, and threw it into the hole. Then he filled the well and worked hard to make sure he got rid of it [i.e. the book]. However, when he finished and came back into his house, the book was still on the table. He then had his wife heat the oven ten times, and he threw the book into the glowing fire, closed the oven, and went back inside. Again, the book was still on the table. The man became so enraged that he lost his sanity. The Devil came every night, and he lay there screaming and shouting for the Devil all the time. His wife and children couldn't control him, and some people came to keep watch over him at night.

Eventually, he became quiet enough that they decided to take him to Rold to see a cunning-woman – or cunning-man, I think it was. They had to travel with him at night, and the man from the nearest farm was strong enough to drive with two heavy black horses. He was instructed to take him [i.e. Per Væver] to Per Damborg. My father was a laborer hired for the harvest at that farm during the hay harvest and grain gathering, and Kræn Rytter asked him if he would drive the madman. He agreed. In the evening, after they had had their meals, he harnessed the horses, and two men came with him to the house. They

took Per Væver, bound his hands and feet, and laid
him in the back of the wagon like a calf. The two
men did not follow; they only went with him to tie
him up. My father was left alone with him. When
they reached the weak place on the road, the horses
stopped, and my father could not get them to move.
He didn't know what to do. He went to the horses,
removed the headgear from one of them, and looked
through it. He saw that there was a person sitting
on the wagon, which made it too heavy. He put the
headgear back on the horses, took his knife from his
pocket, opened it, and drove it firmly into the [horse's]
tail. Then he sat on the wagon, and now he could
drive; the man fell off. He managed to get between
Svendstrup and Ljerre (Lere), in a valley whose name
I can't remember. It was already late at night. Then
three unshorn horses with bells on each came, but
he couldn't see their heads. They couldn't get to the
wagon because of the knife, but they circled it, and
the horses were frightened, so he had to manage them
firmly. When he saw they couldn't get control over
him, he drove on until he reached Rold. Per Væver
lay in the wagon, writhing and shouting for the Devil
all the time, but when Per Damborg came to him, he
calmed him down by reading [texts], and then my
father drove him back home.

The return trip went well. He was still mad,
but the dog was gone and did not return. However,
a glowing wheel began to circle around the house
every night. Per Væver didn't live much longer after
that, and when he died, his wife and children had to

sell the house and move out. It was then dismantled and moved, and the same house still stands today in Restrup Garden, where the gardener lives.
Lars Hansen Dun, Sønderholm.

✕

58. A girl worked for a miller out in the Struer area. The old woman there was ill and couldn't die. One day, when the girl was working in the brew-house, the old woman handed her a book and asked her to burn it. She warned the girl that if she didn't burn it, she would never be able to leave the mill as long as she lived. The girl took the book, but couldn't get it to ignite. One day, her mother came to visit her, and the girl told her about the book, which she had hidden in her chest of drawers. "Let me see it," said the mother. She took the book with a pair of fire tongs and put it in the fire, but it jumped out just as quickly as she put it in. Then she exclaimed, "It's the Devil's work that this book won't burn." Now, the book caught fire and stayed in the flames. Then the old woman died, and they laid her on straw. They always hang something white over the windows when there's a body inside. Two black birds came and perched on the window sills and stayed there the entire time. On the day she was buried, the birds followed along to the cemetery, and when the people carried the body through the gate, the birds flew up into the air and screeched. After that, the girl became ill, and she died fourteen days later. The people at the mill were kind to her in the meantime because they had promised that she wouldn't leave the mill.

Klemen Kristensen, Løgsted.

✕

59. I wanted to get hold of a *Cyprianus*, and when I heard that an old parish clerk had it, I went to ask for it three times, but he gave evasive answers. A good friend of mine said to me, "I have an uncle who owned it, but he couldn't get rid of it. He threw it in the stream at Turebyholm, but when he came home, it was back in its place. He then tried to throw it in the oven, but it was there just the same." So, I gave up on it. A miller's apprentice here at Todbjærg mill did manage to get rid of it, though. He burned it one night because he could resist the temptation when the devilry began.

Sjælland. Hans Nielsen, Todbjærg.

✕

60. There was a man east of Åstrup, they called him Anders Østergård, and he also had a *Cyprianus*. When he died, it was placed under his head in the coffin. His wife asked him, while he was sick, what she should do with it. "You might as well put it under my head in the coffin. There's no point in trying to burn it, because you'll still have it anyway."

Jensine Hansen, Madum Lake.

✕

61. There was a man in Gjæstelev-Lunde renowned for his good deeds, and he could undo any enchantment if they [i.e. clients] came to him immediately. Once, a man from Svanninge visited him because of such an illness. During his visit, he saw an opportunity to take a book from him. The cunning-man let him take it home, but as soon as he arrived there and had removed his head covering, such a restlessness came over him that he had to leave immediately, bareheaded, and return from Svanninge to Gjæstelev-Lunde, which is between two and three miles, to return the book. Only then did he find peace.
Christensen.

X

62. A man in Rahkeby possessed a *Cyprianus*, and to harm another man, he placed the book on a walkway that the man had to cross. The book was laid open, facing the direction from which the man would come. The intention was that the man would step on the book, trip, and injure himself. However, when the man got wind of the plan, he picked up the book instead. He then sold it to a miller's apprentice for eight *riksdaler*, but the miller's apprentice was afraid to keep the book and gave it away.
T. Kr. Kristensen, Hjorring.

X

63. Smith-Lavs, who was one of Cunning-Mads's best friends, is said to have once owned a *Cyprianus*. His son says that he received it from Mads, but Smith-Lavs himself denies this and refuses to reveal from whom he acquired it. However, he mentioned that he didn't dare keep it for long, as he knew that every tenth owner belonged to the Devil. He managed to get rid of it safely, but he won't say to whom [he gave it]. Nevertheless, he promised me that he would obtain it for me if I agreed to own it and sleep with it on my chest for three Thursday nights, which I agreed to, but Lars [the son?] hasn't brought it to me yet.

P. N.

⚒

64. Per Overlade from Havbro had gone down to visit the old parish clerk here, who was named Storm. Then the clerk says, "You have always been a good friend to me, so you shall have this book." The binding was terribly firm, and Per takes it and leaves. Now these two were both half witchdoctors themselves, and when Per reached Gråsten – a stone where it is said that a church once stood, or at least many burial chambers from the Stone Age – he sat down on the stone and tried to open the book to see its contents. It turned out to be a *Cyprianus*. Now he wanted to return it, but he couldn't; he wanted to put it down, but he couldn't do that either. So, he took it home and kept it for many years. One day, when his wife was not at home, he decided he would burn it, but he couldn't do that either. So, he bled himself and covered the book with blood, and that finally succeeded.

Jens Korregård, Havbro.

4. Reading from a *Cyprianus:* Crows or Other Animals Reveal Themselves

65. There lived a man in Eskildstrup, Søllinge parish, who owned a *Cyprianus.* One day, while he was at church, his son got hold of the book and started reading it. As he read, the entire room filled with crows. But the father sensed something was wrong while he was in church, so he hurried home to read [a text in order to drive] the crows away.
Lars Frederiksen.

※

66. A man was sitting and shaving his beard. Then the boy happened to start reading a book that was lying on the table, and suddenly a whole lot of crows came into the room. The man quickly went out to get some grains to scatter for them, then read back (*læste tilbage*) what the boy had read, and afterward gave him a couple of good slaps.
Iver Larsen, Egtved.

※

67. In the village of Bjørnstrup, Ulstrup parish on Refsnæs, there lived a smallholder who owned a *Cyprianus*. In the room where he kept the book, he was often seen sitting and staring at its fiery red letters, apparently very eager to read, but old Søren says he never read aloud. Now, it happened one day, while

the smallholder was out working, that his wife had
an irresistible urge to become more familiar with the
book's contents. She went in, took it down from the
shelf where it lay (up near the ceiling), and eagerly
began to read. But she hadn't been reading for long
before the entire room filled with a multitude of
ravens and crows, and one of them approached her
and clearly asked what she commanded. She was so
frightened that she couldn't say a single word. The
man, who had sensed that something was wrong, came
rushing home and into the room. He snatched the
book from his wife and began to read. Shortly after,
the entire black flock had disappeared again. The man
then asked her to keep her hands off things that didn't
concern her next time, as her curiosity could easily
have caused a great disaster if he hadn't arrived in time
to prevent it.

Some time later, the man died, and the wife, who
still hadn't recovered from her fear of the *Cyprianus*,
thought it best to get rid of it as soon as possible. So she
immediately took the book from the shelf and threw it
on the fire. But at that very moment, it was back in its
place. This happened three times, each with the same
result. The wife then finally understood that it was
impossible to burn the *Cyprianus*, so she gave up trying
and left the book alone. Besides, says old Søren, it is
not the *Cyprianus* but rather the *Sixth and Seventh Books
of Moses* that contain the greatest secrets. So if anyone
really wants to learn the dark arts, they must carefully
study it, although it is said to be a difficult task.
Povl Hansen, Vallekilde.

X

68. In South Fyen, there lived a squire who was very cunning in an art that no one was supposed to know about. He had gained his wisdom from a large book with red letters, which he kept locked in his desk. But one Sunday, he went to church and forgot to remove the key from the desk. A curious maid, who was in the room to sweep, noticed his oversight and removed the book. She opened it and began to read, though without understanding the meaning. However, as she read, a great flock of crows filled the courtyard, so that both the roof and the yard were covered with them. The squire immediately knew what was happening at home. He quickly left the church. When he got home, he first poured out a bushel of peas into the yard for the gathered birds. Then he went into his room and read [a text to drive away] the crows who disappeared as quickly as they had arrived.

H. Hansen (school teacher), Hjallese.

X

69. Jørgen Hansen in Sotrup owned a *Cyprianus*. One evening, after he had become drunk, he started reading it and kept reading for so long that the room filled completely with crows, which later moved out into the trees in the garden. The next morning, there wasn't a single leaf left on the trees, and the people were very upset about it.

Chr. Hanssen, Nørremølle.

X

70. There was a priest over in Angel who owned
a *Cyprianus.* A young boy named Jakob came to be
educated by him. One day, as the priest was reading,
the boy sneaked up behind him and began reading
the book over his shoulder. The priest asked if he was
interested in learning what was written there. The boy
eagerly said yes. So, the priest taught him, and it was
indeed from the *Cyprianus.*

One day, while the priest was at church, the boy
got hold of the book himself and began reading it on
his own. Then an owl flew into the room, followed
shortly by another, and then more, and they flew
around the room. The boy continued reading, and
then a toad came hopping in, followed by another,
until there was a whole group of them. When they
were gone, and he kept reading, snakes began to
appear, and soon there were many of them as well.
Meanwhile, the priest was in the pulpit but noticed that
an owl kept flying outside the window. He understood
that something must be wrong at home, so he hurried
back as fast as he could and arrived in the study just
as the whole group of snakes came slithering out. The
boy, now terrified, had put the book down and didn't
know what to do. The priest immediately saw what
had happened and began to read everything back,
which drove the creatures away. The priest told the boy
that he should thank God that he [i.e. the priest] had
arrived so quickly, for if the snakes had disappeared,
the troll himself would have come, and there would

have been no help for him. The priest then taught him how to read them back.

The boy stayed with the priest and inherited the book after him, though I can't remember exactly how he used it.

When Jakob grew old, he could make the Devil appear whenever he wanted. One day, his son asked if he could see him [i.e. the Devil]. So, one day, they were out by the road digging, and Jakob told him to pay attention, for the Devil would pass by that afternoon. Several people walked by, and eventually, a fine gentleman passed. When he had just passed, the old man asked, "Did you see him?" – "See whom?" – "Him, the one you wanted to see." – "Yes, but where is he?" – "Didn't you see him pass by here?" The son quickly turned around, but there was no-one to be seen. *Lorens Hansen, Fælsted.*

⚸

71. In Als, there was once a priest who was skilled in sorcery. The maid who cleaned the priest's room had a habit of reading his books whenever she could get away with it. One day, while the priest was at church, she noticed a small book with a red cover that she hadn't seen before, and she immediately began reading it. Shortly after, a few flies started buzzing around the room, and the longer she read, the more flies there were. The priest, meanwhile, sensed something was wrong; he stopped in the middle of his sermon and hurried home. He took a large mirror and threw it on the floor, shattering it into countless pieces, then snatched the book from the maid and began to read back everything she had read aloud. Meanwhile, the flies started to piece the mirror back together, and by the time the priest had finished his reading, the mirror was almost completely restored. If the flies had finished their work before the priest had completed his reading, the maid would have been doomed. As it was, the flies had to retreat.

$$\mathbb{X}$$

72. There was a woman from the Bind region who lived in Øster-Lindet, and she had worked for a priest who owned a *Cyprianus*. She was supposed to go in and dust the books. But she wasn't allowed to touch the *Cyprianus*. Still, she was very eager to see it, and one day, she managed to get hold of it and began reading it. Suddenly, the room swarmed with hens and roosters, mostly large black cockerels. She didn't know what to do, but then she started reading from the end of the book, hoping to reverse what had happened. However, it was of no use. The priest noticed what was going on, came in, and picked up another book. As he calmly read aloud, the roosters disappeared just as quickly as they had appeared.
Kjøbenhoved.

$$\mathbb{X}$$

73. My mother had an old aunt who traveled with lace to Als. One day, she arrived at a place where she wanted to lodge, where there were two elderly women, and they owned a *Cyprianus*. They had a little servant girl working for them, and while she was there, the two old women one day ended up reading so much that there were so many flies in the room with them that they couldn't stay there because of them. The girl had to run over to Nørre Herred to fetch a priest, and he came and read, and then the flies disappeared. Later, when my aunt came there, the girl started talking to her about it: "Oh dear, do you dare stay here?" Yes, she did, and she didn't notice anything either.

Ane Marie Møller, Bovlund.

⋊⋉

74. There was a man out on Hanstholm named Jens Vinter, who had received a *Cyprianus* from an old woman and one day sat down to read it. Then a large black dog came in through the door and stood there staring at him with big eyes. The man wanted to chase it out, but the dog resisted him. He found this strange and went back to reading, but the dog seemed so odd to him that he stood up again and went outside to feed the livestock, thinking the dog would disappear. But when he came back inside, the dog was still sitting in the same place. He became fearful of reading the book and wanted to put it back on the shelf. But he couldn't make the dog leave. Just then, an old fisherman named Ole Bjørn came in. He had come from Norway some time ago and settled there [i.e. in Hanstholmen]. When he saw what was happening, he began to read over the dog and managed to get it to leave. Then he said to Jens Vinter, "It's not worth reading that book, for it's a dangerous one. You should let me have it, or else you might end up in worse trouble." Jens Vinter was happy to get rid of the book.

Hansen (school teacher), Vester-Hornum.

✗

75. There was a man in Vilsted who also read in the *Cyprianus.* But as he read, a black cat came to him and stayed with him wherever he went, whether he was sitting, lying down, or walking – the cat was always there, and it drove him nearly mad. He eventually came to Løgstør windmill, where there was a farmhand they called Jens Knægt, whom I knew well. Jens took the book from him, and after that, the man was also free of the cat. However, he never fully recovered from having read that book; every year around Midsummer, he would fall seriously ill. There was a woman down in Vindblæs named Maren Hånning, who was known to be very cunning, but even she couldn't cure him of it, which I found surprising. I didn't think much of Jens Knægt's abilities, but perhaps he was more cunning than I thought.

Niels Kr. Jensen, Fredbjerg.

✗

76. There lived a very cunning woman in Råbjerg, and she also owned a *Cyprianus*. One day, she accidentally summoned the Devil but couldn't banish him. From that time on, he followed her wherever she went, taking the form of a small black poodle. No one could drive him away, no matter how many people she asked for help. Finally, a priest managed to do it, but the woman didn't live a single day after that. It is said that this was the same priest who once made the Devil leave through a knothole in the window at Kjærgård's mill.
H. A. B.

𝕏

77. On a farm near Bavn in Ræær, there was a *Cyprianus*. One day, a neighboring man sent a request to borrow a book from that farm, and by mistake, he was given the *Cyprianus*. Without thinking much about it, he started reading it, and the more he read, the more he wanted to continue. But shortly after he began, a large black poodle came in and lay down under the stove. He started having bad thoughts and stopped reading, but wherever he went afterward, the black dog was always on his heels. A neighbor, to whom he confided his troubles, realized that it was the Devil himself, so they had to send for the cunning-man in Nors. After much effort, the cunning-man managed to banish the dog, and the spot where it happened is still pointed out, lying near the parish boundary between Torp and Hansted fields.
J. G. Pinkolt.

Ж

78. There was a miller in Farstrup Mill who served as a shepherd. One day, he went to visit the priest, and while they were walking around the priest's garden and various things, the priest threw out a certain vulgar book (*kanallibog*) into his garden because he no longer wanted it. The miller was quite curious and noticed the book, so he tucked it under his coat. When he got home, he began reading it both day and night. That evening, as they were eating their dinner, someone came to the door and said, "Søren Pedersen!" The miller was somewhat hard of hearing, but he could hear it well enough, so he went and opened the door, then returned to his chair. Soon, a vulgar person (*kanalli*) came in and went straight to lay its head on his lap. He was startled by this strange creature, which appeared to him as a black dog, but he was only a simple lad of ten years and thought it was just a dog. He opened the door again and followed the creature out to the mill pond, trying to get rid of it, but couldn't separate from it. Then, a man on a horse came, named Anders Ilder, who lived in Hvorup, and was somewhat of a fortune-teller. He later moved to Næsborg. He managed to handle the situation properly. Meanwhile, the miller had been standing in the mill pond, screaming and calling for help, as he had summoned the Devil himself but hadn't learned how to banish him. The miller was known for wanting to take more than his share of people's grain. This incident happened while I served there; I will never forget it.
Povl Thomsen, Havbro.

〤

79. One day, a miller was walking on the mill dam [i.e. on the ice] and found an incredibly beautiful book there. He picked it up and went into his inner room to read it. While he was sitting and reading, a large black dog came in and sat down by his feet on the floor, staring up at him intently. The miller's family couldn't understand what had happened to him, so they went to look for him. When they found him, he was sitting there looking as pale as a corpse. They then sent for a witchdoctor, who came with a man named Hendrik Smid. The witchdoctor managed to banish the Devil and threw the beautiful book back onto the mill pond, just where it had been found. But the book remained inside. One day, when they were baking, they decided to throw the book into the oven and burn it. However, it stayed perfectly in its place on the shelf among the other books, even though it had been burned. So, he went back to the witchdoctor and complained that the ugly book had found its way into his house, and he couldn't get rid of it. The witchdoctor told him to seal the book and put it on the shelf as it was. Since then, the book was never read again.

Jensine Hansen, Madum Lake.

〤

80. Peder Ginderup was known to lend his butter over in Pederstrup. A man named Jokum, who lived in Skals, sent a request to Peder Ginderup to borrow

the *Cyprianus.* He lent it to him but strictly forbade him from reading it, which Jokum promised he would not do. However, while traveling to Hørup Mill, Jokum took a detour to Lovelbro to pick up the book. As he was heading home and had reached Holmgård, he started reading it. His horses then became exhausted and sweaty and could no longer pull the cart. When he looked back, he saw a large black dog lying in the cart. Finally, when he arrived at Skals, where the road passed by Jokum's farm, he stood outside waiting for him. Jokum saw what was happening, grabbed the book, and read from it, causing the dog to disappear. Jokum was a very knowledgeable man and treated many people for various ailments. Whenever cattle were sick, people always went to him.
Ole Lavrsen, Norskov.

5. Reading from a *Cyprianus* and Summoning the Devil

81. It is reliably reported about a miller from Dråby, Horns Herred, that he possessed a *Cyprianus* and could summon the Devil. However, whenever he did so, he always required the presence of two strong men. One day, a man came to him and reported that ten *daler* had been stolen from him at the market and wanted to know who had taken them. At that time, the miller had a threshing man with him. The miller asked him to see if he had noticed anything unusual, and this is how the story goes:

The miller took out his *Cyprianus* and began to read from it. Suddenly, the door flew open, and a large, heavy bull entered. The miller stood up and banged on the table, saying, "What kind of appearance is this today? I suggest you come in a more refined manner." The bull then disappeared, and the miller started reading again. Shortly afterward, the door flew open again, and a soldier entered, dressed in the finest clothes and with the most refined manners one could imagine. "That's more like it," said the miller, "so that one can be properly acquainted with you." The Devil was then asked about the ten *daler*. He was able to provide the information easily because the thief was a close relative of the victim. After giving this correct information, the Devil vanished; but the threshing man sat there, terrified, not knowing if [the Devil] would come or go. This was the last time the miller used the *Cyprianus*, as his wife suffered so much from nightmares

at night that she persuaded him to abandon such practices.
Anna Stolpe.

〤

82. In Torring, East Tørslev Parish, there once was a blacksmith who had a bad habit of drinking. In the evenings, he would sit at the Torslev inn and drink until he could no longer walk, at which point they would throw him out. It often happened that he was seen running away in the form of a hare. One evening, a man who had just returned from the King's service came to the blacksmith's house. The blacksmith was not at home, but the man saw a *Cyprianus* lying in the room. He began to read from it, and then the Devil appeared before him. The man fled through the door with the Devil in pursuit. He ran through all the puddles and dung holes in Torring in his stockings to escape, and only managed to get away when the blacksmith returned and read [a text to drive] the Devil away.
Sofie Lund.

〤

83. Old Rasmus relates: "One evening, while I was living in Østbirk, a traveling grinder came to me and asked for shelter for the night. This man could indeed do more than recite the Lord's Prayer, but that was no surprise, as he possessed a *Cyprianus*. He offered to

sell me the book and to teach me how to understand it, but I replied that he first had to show me if it was any good. I had a hoe that I suspected had been stolen, and if he could retrieve it for me, I would not only believe that the book was effective, but I would also purchase it. He was immediately willing to do so, asked me to follow him outside, and then began to read from the book. Instantly, a large shaggy dog with red, glowing eyes appeared and asked the grinder what he commanded. 'I command you to tell me who has stolen Rasmus's hoe'. 'It is not stolen', said the dog, 'but some boys took it one day and threw it into the mire by the road yonder for fun'. The man read again, and the dog disappeared. The hoe was indeed found at the place the dog had indicated, but I was so frightened of that dog, which was the Devil himself, that I neither dared to keep the book nor to learn such conjurations."
Th. J.

X

84. A cunning-man in Sønderhå was sitting at his table and couldn't go anywhere because he was visited by the Devil, whom he had summoned. To get rid of him, he sent for Hans Plovmand in Skyum. However, Hans replied that it was not urgent; let him be burdened with the Devil a bit longer. Eventually, he came and drove the Devil away. "Now I've dealt with him twice," said Hans, "if he comes a third time, I'll get the Devil with a rod."
Lars Peter Eriksen, Hassing.

✶

85. One night at midnight, my father and mother and I were just north of Lund, near the inn in Bjerget. There came a little pig or something white like a pig running along the roadside. It tried to get up on the side of the road but didn't manage to. We wanted to approach it, but as it came closer, we didn't dare. We walked a bit further and came around a hill where something was burning. We didn't like that and continued walking. Then we came to a place where some men were sitting and reading in the *Cyprianus*. Suddenly, a whole bunch of rags fell down onto their heads, which my parents saw, but I didn't. There was also some scuffling on the roof. Then they sent for the priest, who came and laid three books on the table. He took one and started reading from it. It was the Devil they had summoned, and he had such strength that he threw the first book away from the priest. Then the priest took the second book, and the Devil did the same with it. The third book, however, the Devil could not throw away, and the priest kept reading until he banished the Devil through the window. The man then said they should let a sow out, because as soon as he got outside, he would take whatever he first encountered. The sow was also taken, and they never saw it again.
North Vissing.

✶

86. Once, Anders Høgsgård and Jens Højbjærg (who died in 1868) were traveling to Lemvig. One of them had the horse, and the other had the cart; they had set up camp, as we say. When they were heading home again, they wanted to go quickly because they'd had a little drink. Suddenly, Anders Høgsgård's horse collapsed, and they were stuck. He jumped off the cart, but Jens Højbjærg remained seated. Anders Høgsgård went off to the roadside and called the Devil to him. Meanwhile, Jens Højbjærg was complaining, "What's going to happen here? We need to get going; we can't just sit here." "Shut up!" Anders Høgsgård shouted. He then went to the horse, stroked its back three times, took hold of its mouth, and managed to get the horse up. They continued their journey in haste. The horse could now endure the ride, and they traveled as fast as they needed. It was commonly believed that the man knew more than his Lord's Prayer.

Sø (school teacher), Gudum.

꘡

87. Kristian Vestergård in Høgsted had an appointment with the Devil. He had obtained the *Cyprianus* and was reading it. Then a man came in and asked him what he needed. Kristian said he needed feed and grain, of which he had none. Now, this man usually provided money, and since Kristian Vestergård had no further use for him, the Devil grabbed his head and twisted it around, so he remained a "windhead" (or some say "wind-nosed") for the rest of his life. He

should not have summoned the Devil when he no longer needed him.
Mogens Kristensen, Guldager.

※

88. Mr. Lavrs in Voldum had a servant who was very inquisitive. He often stole into the vicar's private chamber when the priest was not present and read the books there. One day, he stood on a chair in Voldum Church. The servant had managed to get hold of the *Cyprianus* and had come across the red letters, and then he had summoned the Devil. When the priest came in, he took the book from the servant, gave him a good slap, and then took a pin and made a hole through the window frame. He then began reading backwards in the book, and the Devil had to go out through the hole.
Vrinders.

※

89. A priest in Stauning, Pastor Brøllund,[19] was cunning and had attended the Black School, but still belonged to the holy priests. One day, while he was standing in the pulpit, he suddenly ended his sermon and went straight home. His maid had been cleaning his room and had become curious. She had ended up reading in the *Cyprianus* and had summoned the Black

---

19 One of the few identifiable priests in these narratives, Lars Graversen Brøllund (d. 1818) served the parishes of Stadil and Stauning.

Man (*sorte mand*). The priest then banished him [the Devil], gave her [the maid] a stern reprimand, and said that if he had not arrived, it would have cost her her life.

Niels Madsen Holm, Øster Lem.

✸

90. A man in Astrup was reading a book he had received, and then he couldn't sleep or find any rest at night. He wandered around the fields during the night. The priest in Breum cured him so that he could rest and sleep again.

Maren Skade, Åsted.

✸

91. There were two men, Kristen Torholm and Jens Nymark, who were lying up in the hills reading their books. A neighbor heard them reading. One said, "Come!" and the other said, "We should stop reading now." It was probably the Devil they were reading to, for they were the ones who went around bewitching everything in the area.

Dorte Lavstdatter, Hesselbakke.

✸

92. In a place over in Hørmested, called Tørholmhuset, there was a woman named Kirsten Tørholm. She had a son named Kristen, and one day while she was away in town, he got hold of her books and wanted to look at them. Then a stranger came to him and asked what he needed. Kristen did not know, as he had not called for anyone and did not need any help. The stranger then attacked Kristen, splitting both his nose and mouth, and tortured him terribly. Meanwhile, the mother noticed there was a stranger in the house, and when she returned home, she drove the Devil away. But Kristen was never right again and died shortly after.

Kristen Frederiksen, North Bindslev.

※

93. My great-grandfather had borrowed a *Cyprianus* from Trindtveden in Dronningborg. The first thing he read, his vision turned black, and after that, he could see nothing more and thus could not make use of the book. When people came in, he was crouched in the corner of the bench. They quickly sent for the man from whom he had borrowed the book in Trindtveden. When he arrived, he threw open the door to the room, grabbed the book, and said: "Where you entered, there you shall depart." Then he began to read to the Devil, but it was in vain. The people in the room saw nothing, but the Devil did leave, and my great-grandfather was freed and was able to come out of his hiding place.

Jens Mosen, Øster Brønderslev.

※

94. The grandfather of Bødker-Marian's father was a miller at Lindegårds Mill, and he owned a *Cyprianus*. One day, a man came to the mill, and while his sack was being ground, he went into the miller's living room. There was a shelf with books up by the ceiling; he reached up, took one down, and began to read. But it was the *Cyprianus* he had got hold of, and as he sat reading, the room grew thick and dark. They had to send for the miller, who came running in, snatched the book from the man, and gave him a proper thrashing, saying: "Couldn't you keep your nose out of things that don't concern you!"

K. M. Rasmussen.

Ж

95. My mother had an aunt who worked for the farmers in Strandby. One Sunday morning, she was supposed to sweep the rooms and the school while the people were at church. As she was sweeping, a few books fell down from a shelf. She gathered them up, and then she found one open with red letters on each page saying: "Read on!" The girl was only half-grown and started reading the book, thinking it was wonderful to see such a message. But then she remembered she needed to hurry and finish cleaning. When she looked around, the room was as dark as night, with sparks flying around her. As soon as she looked at the book, it was bright enough for her to see. At that moment, the schoolmaster came running in, snatched the book from her hand, and slapped her on the cheek. As soon as he left, the room became a little brighter and brighter, and eventually, she was able to finish cleaning. She promised never to come across such a book again. But it was also not surprising that he would place such a book where someone could easily come across it.

Niels Kr. Jensen, Fredbjærg.

⚔

96. A stranger had stayed overnight at Vestergård, and it was his *Cyprianus* that he had ended up reading. He noticed that Kristen Vestergård was in trouble and came back to help him by getting the other man out of the way.

Linderup.

⚔

97. There was a churchwarden in Harboøre who was to preach in the priest's absence. He was unmarried but had a housekeeper. One day, while he was preaching, she came in and got hold of the *Cyprianus*, and then the Devil appeared and asked what she wanted. She didn't know what to say. The churchwarden realized something was wrong at home, so he rushed down from the pulpit, went home, and drove the Devil away. It was a common belief among people that he [i.e. the churchwarden] would live for a certain period, and then the Devil would come and take him away, body and soul. He also disappeared,

and no one knew what happened to him.
K. N. Norby, Hygum.

)X(

98. In Stadil near Ringkjøbing, there once was a priest who owned a *Cyprianus*.[20] One day, while the priest was at church, he left the *Cyprianus* open on his desk. The maid, who was supposed to clean the room while the priest was away, saw the open book and began to read it. However, she didn't know how to read it correctly and ended up summoning the Devil by mistake. The maid was terrified and couldn't move from the spot. The priest had ascended the pulpit when the maid inadvertently summoned the Devil, and he immediately stopped his sermon and hurried home to the study. There, he began to read from the book himself, forcing the Devil to leave right away.
Maren Bonde, Vedersø.

)X(

99. A girl from Grønning, who was named Ma' Laster, was in service in Lundø. One day, while her master and mistress were at church, the daughter and the maid stayed at home. The maid was very curious about books and found one that had come out of the man's cupboard. She read a bit in it and saw a line that said: "If you want to speak with Mikkel, then turn around."

---

20 Presumably the same Pastor Brøllund mentioned above, see note 18.

At that moment, the daughter came in, looking as red as blood. She gave the maid a good smack, grabbed the book, and said, "You shouldn't be meddling with things that don't concern you." She then put the book back in the cupboard. The maid asked, "Why couldn't I keep reading?" The daughter replied, "Because it was the *Cyprianus*, and you could have read so much that we could have ended up in trouble." It was indeed true, that it happened in this way. Maren Larsdatter [i.e. Ma' Laster] herself told me this.

Peder Hansen, West Grønning.

6. Reading from a *Cyprianus*: The Devil Performs Sundry Work

100. Peder Hanberred, who lived on Stensbæk heath in Bindslev, could summon the Devil and made him carry water in a tub.
Kristian Andersen Hust, Skoven.

⚔

101. Pastor Niels Lang in Vilslev had a servant who, though fully grown, was still called a "youth" because he had been with the pastor's family since the time of Lang's father and brother. This gave him a lot of freedom and sometimes made him curious. One Sunday, he got hold of the *Cyprianus* and read from it until a goose came in and perched on his shoulder, intending to peck him in the face. The pastor's wife heard the servant's screams and guessed what was happening when she heard the goose honking. She grabbed her apron full of grain and scattered it around the house, the entrance hall, and the yard, saying: "Peck it!" The pastor, who had just begun his sermon in Vilslev, instead said: "I have an urgent matter to attend to right now at home in Vilslev, which cannot be postponed, so I must leave immediately. Please excuse me." He then hurried home, and he arrived just in time. The servant was driven away and received a stern reprimand.
J. J.

⚔

102. In Hjarup, there was a priest who owned a *Cyprianus* and knew how to use it effectively. One day, the priest in Nagbølle borrowed it from him, but he wasn't as skilled with it. When he read from it, a canary appeared, but he didn't know how to get rid of it. To buy time, he instructed the canary to pull up trees in the garden, but the canary managed this task much more easily than the priest had anticipated, causing the priest great distress about how to handle the situation. Meanwhile, the priest in Hjarup sensed that something was amiss and figured something must be wrong in Nagbølle. He quickly harnessed his horse and drove there. On the way, he met the vicar of Nagbølle's cart, which had been sent to fetch him. Upon arriving and seeing the situation, he immediately threw a bushel of grain into the garden to keep the canary occupied while he retrieved the book and read from it to drive the canary away. He managed to get the book and read in such a way that the canary had to leave.

G. N. Bugge.

⚔

103. Recently, there lived a cunning-man in Fårup known as Mads Hansen, commonly referred to as Cunning-Mads. He possessed both the skill and ability to demonstrate his control over the Devil using the *Cyprianus*. A close acquaintance of Cunning-Mads was Smith-Lars from Rettestrup. Whenever Lars faced difficulties in treating an animal's illness, he would often refer the case to Mads, believing that the issue might be caused by malevolent forces that Mads was equipped to address. On one occasion, Lars, during a visit to Mads, expressed skepticism about Mads's abilities and challenged him to provide proof of his prowess. Mads agreed to demonstrate his expertise and invited Lars to join him in the attic, where they measured out two bushels of yellow peas. Mads then scattered these peas across the attic floor and asked Lars to hold the sack while he fetched the *Cyprianus* and began reading from it. Immediately, the Devil appeared in the form of a red-haired imp and commenced collecting the peas one by one with great diligence. Within approximately ten minutes, all the peas were returned to the sack. Lars, feeling intense apprehension at being so close to the Devil, was immobilized, with his feet seemingly glued to the floor and his hands gripping the sack tightly. He was only able to move once the task was completed and the Devil dismissed. This experience eliminated any doubts Lars had about Mads's wisdom.

P. N.

※

104. Many years ago, a maid working at Skjeminggård was in her master's room performing her usual duties when she noticed a book lying on his desk. She picked it up and started reading without considering its significance. Suddenly, her master burst in, snatched the book from her, ran up to the attic, and threw a barrel of barley and a barrel of peas into the yard. He then hurried back inside, took the book, and began reading from it. To the girl's horror, she saw that the yard was filled with black ravens, which began to fly away one by one. The master had to recite [from the book] in order to return everything the girl had [conjured] previously by reading from the book. If he could finish reading before the ravens had collected all the barley and peas he had thrown out, he would overcome them. He managed to complete the reading just in time, and the last raven flew away. The master then gave the girl a stern warning to stay away from such matters in the future.

R. Kristensen, Vester Skerninge

X

105. A boy in Rosborg was tending the sheep when he found a book and began reading it. It was a *Cyprianus*, but he ended up reading the wrong section, and then the Devil appeared and asked what he should do. The boy asked him to gather stones from the fields. The Devil scattered the stones in all directions, and the task was soon completed. Then the Devil returned and asked what he should do next. The boy told him to scoop water from a lake with a bottomless sieve. At first, the Devil managed to do this, but soon the water flowed back into the lake, and the Devil had to leave.

Kobberup.

X

106. A man made a pact with the Devil that he would provide him with work for seven years. First, the Devil was tasked with removing all the stones from his field, from the size of a pea and up, and digging three cubits down into the ground. This took him nearly a year to complete. I don't recall what other tasks he was given, but he finished those swiftly as well. When the man was in trouble trying to find more work for him, he accidentally let out a fart and said to the Devil, "Catch that and put it back the same way it came out." The Devil went off to catch it, and he chased after it for the remaining seven years. Every time he got a little bit of it in his grasp, it slipped away again, and he could never fully capture it.

Karen Marie Rasmussen.

𝌴

107. There was a maid whose master and mistress were going to church on a Sunday. The master told her, as he was leaving, that she should spread the manure that was on the field. She was reluctant to do this, so she decided to pass the time by reading the *Cyprianus*, knowing where it was kept. Lucifer came in and asked her what she wanted. She told him she was not interested in doing the work herself and suggested that he spread the manure for her. He did that. When he was finished, he wanted to know what else she wanted him to do. There was a lot of birdseed on their loft that had fallen into the cracks between the beams, and she asked him to collect it. However,

Lucifer couldn't handle birdseed with his fingers; it was forbidden for him. So, since she had nothing more for him to do, he went away, and she was free of him.
Johanne Marie Kristensdatter, Søbeden

)\(

108. In Hedegård, Bindslev, there was a cunning-man. One Sunday, he went to church and forgot to lock his cabinet where he kept his books. A servant, noticing the open cabinet, looked in the books and began reading them. Unfortunately, he also read from the evil book *Cyprianus* and at an unfortunate spot, thus summoning the Devil. The Devil appeared and asked him what he wanted. The servant knew that he could give the Devil three tasks. If the Devil completed all three, he would gain control, but if he failed, he would leave in shame. The servant, knowing what to do, quickly went up to the loft, grabbed a bushel of peas, scattered them on the floor, and instructed the Devil to count and collect them all back into the sack. The Devil managed to do this quickly. The servant then asked what else he should do. Next, he instructed the Devil to go to the field and spread the manure that had been left there. Meanwhile, the man in church sensed something was wrong and quietly left. When he arrived home, he saw the entire field covered in a thick fog of dust and manure. He hurried inside, grabbed the book, and read [from the book in order to drive] the Devil away. Afterward, he gave the servant a thorough scolding.
Martin Iversen, Kvissel.

X

109. On a Sunday, a man from Hedegård told his maid before going to church that she must not look at the book on the desk when she went in to clean. Despite this, she glanced at the book and read a small part of it. As a result, the Devil appeared and asked what he should do. She instructed him to spread the manure that was piled up in the yard, which amounted to about a hundred loads. The Devil went to work, but when the maid peeked out to see how things were going, the manure flew up into the air and fell over the entire Bindslev parish. When the man returned from church, he saw the mess and rushed home in a hurry. He quickly read a passage from the book to banish the Devil, and the Devil left.

Kristian Andersen Hust, Skoven, Bindslev.

X

110. A man in Tolne owned a *Cyprianus*. One day, while he was out of town for a short while, his daughters found the book because he had forgotten to lock the cupboard where it was kept. The girls began to read from it, but unfortunately, they read the part that summoned the Devil. The Devil appeared immediately and asked what he should do. One of the daughters, showing remarkable presence of mind, ordered him to spread a large amount of manure that was piled up on the field. The Devil went to work, but he spread the manure in the air, making a tremendous mess. The man saw what was happening and realized that something was wrong. He hurried home and managed to arrive before the Devil finished with the manure, allowing him to read [from the *Cyprianus* in order to drive] the Devil away. Despite this, the damage was considerable. One daughter died soon after from the fright, and the other went mad for the rest of her life. *L. C. P.*

✕

111. The Devil once cried, and this is how it happened: There was a girl who wished she could go to church one day, but her master wouldn't allow her as she had to spread manure [on the fields]. There were, as I recall, several loads of manure on the field that she was supposed to spread. She got hold of a *Cyprianus* and began to read from it, and soon the Devil appeared and asked what she commanded. The girl, weary of spreading the manure herself, asked the Devil to do it. He went out and worked with the manure so violently that it flew high into the air. He soon finished this task and came back to ask what he should do next. The girl wanted to get rid of him but didn't know how to read him away. In a moment of desperation, she plucked a hair from her own body and asked him to straighten it. The Devil couldn't manage it; the more he tried, the more tangled the hair became. In the end, he broke the hair in two, which he wasn't supposed to do, and that made him cry. He had hoped to keep the girl in his power, but he failed.

Karen Marie Rasmussen.

⚔

112. A man made a pact with the Devil that he would grant the Devil his soul in three years, unless he could assign him [i.e. the Devil] a task that he couldn't complete. Time passed, and when the Devil came to claim him, the man remembered that his wife had truly curly hair of the right kind. The Devil asked for the task, so the man plucked a strand of his wife's hair and said, "Can you straighten this?" The Devil worked on it for a long time but couldn't get it straight. Finally, he went to the house's wooden pillar, bored a hole in it, inserted the hair, and placed a stick in the hole, thinking that would make it straight. But when he pulled the hair out, it was still as curly as ever. The Devil grew furious, tossed the hair onto the man's bed, and said, "There it is. I can't straighten it." With that, he left and never returned.

N. J. Termansen.

⚔

113. My father once told a story about a man in Sødring who had dealings with the Devil. One day, the Devil came and asked what he should do. The man, in a panic and unable to think of anything quickly, was in a desperate situation. However, there was an old woman sitting by the stove who reached up under her skirts and pulled out a strand of hair from her body. She handed it to the Devil and said, "Straighten this out, if you can!" The Devil tried his best to stretch and straighten the hair, but it was curly and remained so no matter what he did. He couldn't straighten it, so that piece of work had to be abandoned.

Karen Marie Rasmussen.

✳

114. Once there was a farmer who made a pact with the Devil. The agreement was that if the farmer couldn't come up with any more work for him [i.e. the Devil], he would belong to the Devil. The farmer had a rugged farm, full of stones, ditches, swamps, and bogs, so he thought the Devil would have plenty to do. However, as time went on and the work progressed, the farm was improved: the land was leveled, stones were removed, ditches were filled, and the bogs were drained. Once everything was in good order and the farmer couldn't think of anything more for the Devil to do, the Devil came rushing and demanded, "What should I do now?" The farmer said, "Wait a bit, let me think for a moment." But the Devil kept insisting, and the farmer, unable to come up with anything, was scratching his head and beard. Then he noticed that a very curly hair had come off his beard. He got the idea to say, "You can straighten this hair for me." The Devil grabbed the hair and tried to smooth it out, but no matter how hard he worked on it, it remained as curly as ever. Finally, he left in frustration and never returned to the farmer.

Anton Nielsen

⚹

115. The deceased cottager Hans Hansen from Svendstrup, commonly known as Tindre-Hans H.[ansen] because of his favorite expletive, "The Devil strike me (*F. tindre mig*)," served as a farmhand for a bachelor in Rettestrup, who was known only by the name Mads Basherumpe. It was well-known that Mads had a clear association with the Devil himself. Mads often went out and came home late at night. Sometimes the workers were still up, but sometimes they had already gone to bed. It was strictly forbidden to help with harnessing the horses or to be seen around the yard once the horses were stabled. At first, Hans thought Mads's rules were [laid down] merely out of a desire to avoid burdening his workers with the task. Despite this, Hans would sneak out to help harness the horses. However, he soon saw Mads standing calmly with his hands in his pockets, whistling, while a remarkably large ram sprang around the horses, harnessing them. From then on, Hans stayed well inside when Mads came back to the farm.

P. N.

⚹

116. Tindre-Hans, while working for Mads Basherumpe, had to deal with many difficult assignments, and it was rare for him to be done before late at night, especially when covering distances of about three miles. One evening, as he returned home, he found the gate wide open. When he stopped, the familiar gray ram began removing the harnesses. Hans didn't immediately notice what the ram was doing and assumed it had accidentally wandered out of the sheep pen. He hurried to close the gate, wrapped the ram around the waist, and dragged it back to its companions. While doing this, Hans heard a suppressed chuckling. When he returned to the horses, the ram was still there, continuing to harness them. It became clear to Hans who he had been dealing with. Only when he was back in his own room, with the blanket over his head, did he feel somewhat relieved. However, the barn was adjacent to his room, and soon there was a tremendous racket coming from it. All the firewood that had been neatly stacked was being hurled against the wall next to Hans's bed with great force. Hans listened to the commotion for a while, thinking it would stop soon, but it only got worse. After a quarter-hour of relentless noise, he finally became very angry, jumped out of bed, and went to Mads to hold him responsible for the disturbance. He threatened to leave immediately if it didn't stop. Mads Basherumpe just laughed at Hans's threats and told him to go back and lie down, which Hans did. The noise ceased immediately. The next day, when Hans couldn't resist checking the barn, he found all the firewood untouched, exactly as it had

been before, as if nothing had happened.
P. N.

𝕏

117. It was not only in the guise of the gray ram that
the Devil was tasked with labor at Mads's farm; he also
appeared in other forms to Hans. Mads had instructed
Hans not to feed the horses in the evening or to enter
the feed loft after work. Despite this, Hans sometimes
felt it was a shame to let the horses go hungry after
a long day, so he took it upon himself to disobey his
master's orders and fed the horses anyway. However,
when Hans tried to leave, the feed chest, which was
kept in the loft, came after him and jumped onto his
back. Startled, Hans quickly fled through the door, and
he could clearly hear the chest laughing triumphantly
inside the loft as if celebrating its victory over him.
P. N.

𝕏

118. Smith-Lars from Rettestrup had apprenticed
with the cunning blacksmith in Fårup, who owned a
Cyprianus. One time, when Lars was home visiting in
Rettestrup and was returning to Fårup at night, he
noticed with surprise that there was a fire in the smithy.
He sneaked around the smithy and into a small house
that was used for standing in when the horses were
being shod. There was a hole bored in a post, and
through this hole, Lars saw his former master standing

inside the smithy. A small white-haired boy was working with a large hammer.

Wherever the master pointed, the boy had to strike, and the next morning, Lars found that there were 100 more horseshoes in the smithy than when he had left home. This master always had the precision he aimed for. Even though he was somewhat fond of drinking, he could always win prizes in target shooting and hit the bullseye, no matter how drunk he had been beforehand.

P. Nielsen (school teacher), Skuderløse.

⚒

119. Esben knew well that every other line in a *Cyprianus* was red, and he also knew that Hans Smid, who lived on Svinø and later moved to Kjøng, owned this book. People came from near and far to seek his advice. One morning, when Esben passed by the smithy very early, the door was closed. But he saw smoke rising from the chimney and heard an unusually loud hammering on the anvil. Curious, he crept closer to the smithy's door and peeked through a crack. He saw a dwarf-like, red-haired figure striking powerfully with the largest sledgehammer on the glowing iron, while the master, with a small hand hammer, indicated how it should be struck. The dwarf stood on a platform to better reach. Esben believed that it must be the Devil himself working there.

P. N.

)(

120. My grandfather was a blacksmith and lived in Fovling parish. His smithy was located a bit outside the village. One night, when it was quite dark, he was on his way to the smithy with the key to the door in his pocket. On the way there, he saw that the smithy was lit up, and he could hear the sound of hammering inside. He continued on, put the key in the lock, and opened the door, but there was no one inside.

Hans Jæger, Hunderup.

)(

121. A Swede named Niels Hest, who was very strong, was threshing rye on Amager and was to be paid by the barrel. He asked how many barrels he was expected to thresh per week and was told that he could thresh as many as he wanted. He threshed twenty barrels a week, while an average man could manage only six barrels. Niels Hest could even stand outside for several hours talking with others. No one was allowed to enter the barn while he was working. One day, when a hatch to the barn was left open, something was read aloud at the hatch, a cross was made, and a lock was placed on it. That night, the barn was locked. When it was opened the next day, a black cat with glowing eyes flew out of the barn. Niels Hest had a severe twitch in his legs and was sick for a period afterward. It was believed that he had the Devil or invisible powers helping him and that he had summoned spirits to do the threshing

for him. In 1880, he drowned in Øresund, and it is said
that the Devil took him.
Jens Rasmussen, Stensby.

X

122. The Devil had entered the service of a thatcher,
agreeing to work for him for seven years without pay
or food, on the condition that he would receive the
thatcher's soul if he could satisfy him. The Devil did
his best but never managed to fully satisfy the thatcher.
Despite the cheap labor, the thatcher kept him on, as
he saved several hundred *daler* a year by doing so. As
the end of the contract approached, the Devil resolved
to work so well that the thatcher would be satisfied.
When they had to thatch the barn at Dønnerupgård,
they left early in the morning. The thatcher said,
"I'm beginning to become satisfied with you, but it's
not as easy to serve a thatcher on a barn roof as on
a farmhouse roof; and I've never had anyone who
could manage it." The Devil thought he could handle
it. They started the work, and it went well with the
two lower rows, but as they went higher, the thatcher
grew hotter and more demanding. He kept shouting:
"Hay, poles, twigs, stuff it in! Get me the jug and let me
drink!" These words buzzed around the Devil's ears so
much that he became completely dizzy and couldn't
think straight or collect himself. He ran away from
the job, and it's uncertain whether or not the thatcher
ended up in heaven.
Chr. Weiss.

7. Reading from a *Cyprianus:* The Devil Empties Lakes, Builds Dams, Earthworks, Bridges, etc.

123. There was a man named Jonas who made fiddles. One Christmas Eve, he went around playing music and also visited Mosegården. At that time, the lady of the house had recently acquired a wicked book and had summoned the Evil One. He asked her what he should do, but she was not very decisive and only asked if he would fetch her husband. No sooner had he [the husband] removed one of his boots, the Devil arrived, and Jonas had to march to Wåst with one boot and one bare foot. When Jonas arrived, the Devil was so worn out that he nearly lost his life. The Devil then asked Jonas what he should do. Jonas said that the Devil should empty the lake at Wåst with a sieve, as the lake is located a bit east of the town. The Devil could not complete this task, and thus they parted ways. Jonas then took back the book and told the lady not to use it again.

The same Jonas could also play the ellefolk's piece, but when he began, someone had to stand by with a knife to cut the strings, otherwise he could not stop, and everything would dance around, including people, animals, and livestock. It was an elleboy up in Rold Forest who had taught him this. When he played, the ellefolk, tiny beings, would dance continuously.
South Kongerslev.

Ж

124. A woman in Møltrup, named Mariane Hywl
(Hjul), was so careless as to read in a wicked book, and
then someone came in and asked what she wanted
from him. She replied that she wanted him to send
for her husband, who was working far out at Randrup
near Skibsted. He arrived hurriedly, wearing one boot
and one bare foot. "Why did you send such a message
for me, dear wife?" he asked. She explained that she
had accidentally read from a book and that someone
had come to her, but she didn't know what to ask him
to do. "You shouldn't have done that," he said. "You
should have made him empty the sea with a sieve."
Karen Jeppesdatter, Brøndbjærg.

Ж

125. At a certain place, they had a *Cyprianus*, and the
man was a witchdoctor. One day he was away from
town, and his wife wanted to read in the evening for
amusement. She got hold of the *Cyprianus*, and at the
end of each page, it read: "Turn the page!" She kept
reading. Eventually, a large black dog appeared. She
was startled, and the dog asked her what she wanted.
"I want you to bring my husband home," she said. The
dog did bring her husband, but he was missing one
boot. The man then told the dog to get him the other
boot. After that was done, the man said again, "Here
is a sieve; now you must go and empty Majum Lake."
The dog couldn't take the sieve, because of course

the slats were crossed, and the Devil cannot handle things that are crossed. Since then, the woman stopped reading the *Cyprianus*.

Jensine Hansen, Madum Lake.

X

126. One of Money-Lavste's maids found a book in his room and, while reading it, summoned the Devil. He asked what he should do. She gave him a sieve and told him to go out and empty the pond. Money-Lavste was not home, but when he arrived, the Devil was there, trying to empty the pond but couldn't get more out of it. Eventually, he managed to get rid of him [the Devil].

Peder Jensen Pedersen, Thomaskjær.

X

127. On a Sunday, the miller's apprentice in Søndermølle, Sevel, was home alone and started looking through some books. He found the *Cyprianus* and summoned the Devil by reading from it. The Devil asked what he should do, and the apprentice, momentarily bewildered, finally said that he should empty the water from the mill pond. The pond was full. While the Devil was working on this task, they sent for the priest, who arrived and recited a text against (*læser for*) the Devil, causing him to disappear. After that, it was noticeable in the pond what work had been done, as it was never as full of water again.

Peder Kristensen, Hvidbjærg.

Ж

128. A miller's apprentice named Mads in Søndermølle, Sevel, had received the *Cyprianus* from a man named Henrik Kokborg and began reading from it. The Devil then appeared and started knocking on the door, but he couldn't get in because he was barred. When the miller himself arrived, he placed his arms on the lower door and invited the Devil in. The Devil entered, but not to the miller; instead, he went up to the millhouse where the apprentice was. Mads, going about his business, was closely followed by the Devil, who kept bothering him with various annoyances. Unable to escape the Devil's presence, Mads consulted Henrik, who was present, on what to do. Henrik advised him to have the Devil empty the mill pond using a sieve without a bottom, and to dump the water on the mill hill just east and north of the pond. If the sieve had had a bottom, the Devil wouldn't have been able to manage the task due to all the crosses created by the slats, but with the sieve being bottomless, it went swiftly for him. Eventually, only a small hole remained in the eastern side of the pond, and that spot is still deep to this day. Old Pastor Bøtcher (the father of Provst B.) was then summoned. He came and managed to banish the Devil, but demanded something in return. They had to allow him to take the hound with him. They could hear it barking as he left with it. After that incident, the apprentice was never quite the same again.
Jakob Kristensen, Ry College.

⚹

129. One evening, a carpenter named Henrik
Kokborg and some others were in Søndermølle
reading from the *Cyprianus*. Suddenly, the Devil
appeared, and they needed to give him something to
do while they sent for Pastor Bøtcher from Sevel. First,
Henrik Kokborg emptied a bag of feathers into the
wind, and the Devil was tasked with collecting them.
He quickly finished this task, and the priest still hadn't
arrived. Next, he was asked to count the kernels in a
measure of rye. He completed that task swiftly as well,
and then they gave him a sieve with which to empty
the mill pond. This task took him some time. When
the priest arrived, he banished the Devil. However, no
one was allowed to watch, and when someone peeked,
the Devil could not be banished further and was left in
a place where there is a green spot that never freezes
over [in the winter]. Henrik Kokborg was known for
his alleged witchcraft.

Veterinary doctor, Christensen, West Brønderslev.

⚹

130. A maid, who was alone at home, got hold of the
Cyprianus and accidentally read it in such a way that
a figure in dark clothing appeared to her. The figure
asked what she wanted. She responded by saying:
"Take this small bucket and fill it with water." There
was a large tub in the room. The figure continued with
this task until her household returned home. They then

struggled to get rid of him. A priest, who was known for having been born by ceasarean section,[21] was summoned to remove him. However, he was unable to do so. The figure complained, "You have wronged me because you stole a two-*skilling* cake." Indeed, he had done so out of necessity and desperation and threw two *skilling* coins on the ground. The figure then vanished, and the other person also disappeared.

The tub was a large container used, for example, for distilling spirits.

Else Mikaelsdatter, Grindsted.

𝕏

131. To the east of Salling, there is a promontory extending into Limfjord. Nearby lived a man who owned the *Cyprianus.* One Sunday, when he had gone to church and the maid was home alone, she found the book and began to read it. No sooner had she done so than the Devil appeared and asked what she wanted him to do. The poor girl, who was originally from Himmerland and was afraid of the sea voyage, thought it would be nice to go home, so she asked him to build a bridge across the fjord. He set to work, and the hills began to move, dumping soil directly into the fjord. When the people came back from church, and the man understood what had happened, he hurried home and retrieved the book. However, the earth that had been

---

21 Being born by cesarean section was considered an omen presaging magical abilities.

dumped into the fjord remained there and formed the promontory that still exists.

Morten Jeppesen, Tovstrup.

⟨X⟩

132. There was an old cunning-woman in Tise who possessed the *Cyprianus*. One day, while she was at church and her daughter was home alone, the daughter got hold of the book and began to read it. Then the Devil appeared and asked, "What does my master command?" The daughter was quite startled by this but managed to keep her wits about her and said that he should build a road from there to Himmerland. The woman in church could sense that something was amiss, as it was said that she could always tell when something was wrong in such cases, so she hurried home. When she learned what her daughter had commanded, she stopped the work, which is why the causeway was only half built.

The same woman was also once said to have gone to church and instructed her daughter to churn the cream while she was away. She told her to say, "A spoonful from each," when adding the cream to the churn. But the daughter thought that was too little and said, "A ladleful from each." The woman sensed something was wrong and hurried home, only to find that the daughter had cream up to her knees. She had not expected so much cream to come from the churning.

Kristen Mortensen, Risum.

Ж

133. Regarding a spit of land that extends from Salling into Hvalpsund towards Himmerland, the following legend is told: A man once made a pact with the Devil, agreeing that he would belong to the Devil if the Devil could create a piece of land connecting Salling and Himmerland during the time the church service was held at Tise Church. The Devil began his work on a holy day, but he didn't manage to extend further into the fjord than the current spit of land before the people came out of the church.
P. K. Jensen.

Ж

134. In another place, the man of the house was not home, and it was a Sunday during the middle of the sermon. The household staff got hold of the *Cyprianus*, and as soon as they had read a small part of it, someone appeared and asked what task they had for him. In their fright, they told him to build a bridge over the fjord before the priest finished his sermon. However, the man, who was in church, could sense that something was wrong at home. When they told him what had happened, he managed to recite words that sent him [i.e. the Devil] away from him *(læst fra sig)* again. There are good indications that this actually happened, as there is a large spit of land jutting into the fjord, which is called Grønninge Promontory.
Peder Hansen, West Grønning.

𝄪

135. At Hule Mill, there lived a man who owned the *Cyprianus*. One day, the man and his wife went to take communion, leaving the maid alone at home. She got hold of the book, and soon the Devil appeared, eager to be given work. However, she didn't have any tasks for him to do. Eventually, she handed him some tools and told him to create a road through Lund Hills so that they could get to Nibe, and so that people could reach the mill. She thought that this would keep him busy until her master returned home. But even that wasn't enough to occupy him. So, she then tasked him with emptying the mill pond, but only gave him a sieve with which to do it. Unable to complete the task, the Devil had to leave empty-handed. This is how the hollow in the hills was formed.

Jens Mark, Vogslev.

𝄪

136. It is told that one Sunday, when everyone was at church and no one was home at Hule Mill except a girl, she started rummaging through some books and came across the *Cyprianus*. She began to read from it, inadvertently summoning the Devil. Now, she didn't know how to get rid of him, and he claimed her as his own unless she could come up with a task for him to perform. But she couldn't think of anything. Then, she got hold of the miller, who was also home, and he instructed her to have the Devil create a road through the hills. It didn't take long before the road was completed. Then, the miller came up with the idea to have the Devil empty the mill pond using a large potato sieve. The Devil couldn't complete the task and was forced to leave.

Juliane Marie Povlsdatter, Vogslev.

X

137. A girl got hold of the *Cyprianus* and began to read from it. Soon, the Devil appeared and asked her what she wanted from him. Naturally, she became very frightened, but then she thought to tell him that he should throw the heath of Estvedgård into the air while the priest was preaching. It was a Sunday, and she had taken the book down after the people had left for church. So, the Devil began to toss the heath, and the people in the church became alarmed and sent word for the priest to come down from the pulpit. It [i.e. the heath] was originally a large hollow that stretched across the entire heath south and west of Ronbjærg, but it has since diminished greatly. It was said that if the Devil could have overpowered the priest, he would have taken the girl.

Peder Kristensen, Hvidbjærg.

X

138. Legend has it that when Skeel of Benzon was building Veggerslev Vase [a bridge in the area], he couldn't get the work done and therefore made a pact with the Devil, who then completed the work. Skeel was supposed to meet him on the bridge, but he tricked the Devil and didn't show up. The Devil is still waiting for him there. This is where the old saying comes from: "Our Lord is not on Veggerslev Vase." As a boy, I was asked: "Where is Our Lord not?" The answer was always: "On Veggerslev Vase."

J. Y. Nissen, Bamten.

※

139. A servant boy was sent by his master to the priest to borrow a book. On his way back, the boy felt the urge to look inside the book, and once he started reading, he couldn't stop, as if he was compelled. Before he knew it, the Devil appeared in front of him and asked what he wanted. In his fright, the boy answered that he would like the Devil to build a bridge over Kallerup Ford. Immediately, there was a tremendous noise of stones and gravel at the ford, and in just a moment, the bridge was built. The Devil then returned and asked the boy what he wanted next. The boy, still terrified, let out a fart and said to the Devil, "If you can drive that back in where it came from, you can take me, otherwise, you have to let me go." A little later, the Devil came back and said, "No, I couldn't do it. I've traveled across seven parishes and still only managed to get one whip-crack on it." So the boy was set free.

L. N. Bertelsen.

)(

140. On the road from Gjersbøl to Kallerup, just north of Snedsted, there is a ford across Kallerup Stream called Kallerup Ford. All you can see is water and mud, yet people drive across it confidently without sinking through, whereas the sides are bottomless.

A foolish shepherd boy had summoned the Devil and couldn't get rid of him. The Devil asked, "What does my master command?" The boy then told him to turn all the hay in Beersted Bog. This was done immediately, and the Devil asked what else he should do. The boy replied, "Now go and build me a bridge over the stream over there. It must neither be heard nor seen, and it should last forever, so there will never be a need to build another bridge there." The Devil then started in the mountains, and gravel and stones were thrown into the stream. But many of the large stones were also lost along the way, and they are scattered along the road from Gjersbøl across the Kallerup Ford toward Tisted. It's so vivid that you can almost imagine where he set his foot with every single step he took. The boy still wasn't rid of the Devil, but finally, he came up with an idea. He tore off a hair and asked the Devil to put it back where it came from. But the Devil couldn't manage this task; he ran across seven parish boundaries after it and still couldn't even land a single whip-crack. So, he had to admit defeat, and the boy was set free.

P. Uhrbrand.

⋊⋉

141. There was a ferryman at Vilsund who possessed the *Cyprianus*. One day, he had gone to church, and the farmhand, left alone, started rummaging through some papers and found the *Cyprianus*. He began reading it, and soon the Devil appeared, asking what he commanded. The farmhand became deathly afraid and didn't know what to say. Finally, he thought to say, "You can build a bridge over Vilsund." So the Devil rushed away to do just that. When the ferryman returned home, he saw that clay and dirt were piled up in a long line out over the strait, and when he went to investigate, he found the Devil up in the hills, scraping away, causing sand, clay, and gravel to fly everywhere. The ferryman immediately realized what was happening. If a bridge were to be built over the strait, it would be a severe blow to his livelihood. So, he quickly went home, grabbed the book, and summoned the Devil back again, commanding him to leave the bridge alone. The work stopped, but you can still see it today. There's a long tail of land sticking out into the water, as if it had been scraped out. The old folks called it the Devil's Tongue or something like that.
Tøger Dissing, Mors.

⋊⋉

142. My father worked as a ferryman at Vilsund, and he told me about something that happened before his time. One day, the ferryman had gone to church

in Flade, and the farmhand wasn't around, so his daughter was home alone. She took a book from the shelf and started reading it. After she had read a little, a large man entered, and he looked rather ugly: it was the Devil himself. He asked her why she had called him. She said she hadn't called anyone. He insisted that she had called him through the book. She said she didn't know about that. He then asked if she would tell him what he should do. She wasn't sure, but then she asked if he could build a bridge over the fjord. Now, there are large hills at Vilsund, and he went out and started working on the hill, creating a large peninsula that still exists today. Meanwhile, her father came out of the church because he sensed that something was wrong at home. As he walked down the road, he saw a person moving the hills into the fjord, and he realized he had to stop him because he didn't want that work done – it would interfere with his livelihood. So, he went to forbid the Devil from doing the work. But the Devil replied that he had been summoned. The father said he had to give him another task instead. "Just wait a bit," said the father, "let me think of something." Meanwhile, the father had loaded his shotgun, and then he let out a hellish curse and said, "Now, drive this back where it came from." The Devil flew over eighteen church parishes and couldn't catch the curse – he only got a slight graze. So, the Devil gave up; he couldn't catch it. And that's how they got rid of him.
Mads Filtenborg, Stevnstrup.

Appendix

The numbering of each individual legend in this volume, with the corresponding number in Evald Tang Kristensen's *Danske Sagn,* Vol. 6 (Aarhus, 1900), in brackets:

1 (70)	22 (185)	43 (206)
2 (71)	23 (186)	44 (207)
3 (72)	24 (187)	45 (215)
4 (73)	25 (188)	46 (216)
5 (74)	26 (189)	47 (217)
6 (75)	27 (190)	48 (218)
7 (76)	28 (191)	49 (219)
8 (77)	29 (192)	50 (220)
9 (78)	30 (193)	51 (221)
10 (79)	31 (194)	52 (222)
11 (80)	32 (195)	53 (223)
12 (175)	33 (196)	54 (224)
13 (176)	34 (197)	55 (224)
14 (177)	35 (198)	56 (226)
15 (178)	36 (199)	57 (227)
16 (179)	37 (200)	58 (228)
17 (180)	38 (201)	59 (229)
18 (181)	39 (202)	60 (230)
19 (182)	40 (203)	61 (231)
20 (183)	41 (204)	62 (232)
21 (184)	42 (205)	63 (233)

64 (234)   94 (264)   124 (294)
65 (235)   95 (265)   125 (295)
66 (236)   96 (266)   126 (296)
67 (237)   97 (267)   127 (297)
68 (238)   98 (268)   128 (298)
69 (239)   99 (269)   129 (299)
70 (240)   100 (270)   130 (300)
71 (241)   101 (271)   131 (301)
72 (242)   102 (272)   132 (302)
73 (243)   103 (273)   133 (303)
74 (244)   104 (274)   134 (304)
75 (245)   105 (275)   135 (305)
76 (246)   106 (276)   136 (306)
77 (247)   107 (277)   137 (307)
78 (248)   108 (278)   138 (308)
79 (249)   109 (279)   139 (309)
80 (250)   110 (280)   140 (310)
81 (251)   111 (281)   141 (311)
82 (252)   112 (282)   142 (312)
83 (253)   113 (283)
84 (254)   114 (284)
85 (255)   115 (285)
86 (256)   116 (286)
87 (257)   117 (287)
88 (258)   118 (288)
89 (259)   119 (289)
90 (260)   120 (290)
91 (261)   121 (291)
92 (262)   122 (292)
93 (263)   123 (293)

Bibliography

Álvarez, Nicolás. Trans. *Magia Naturalis et Innaturalis: or, Threefold Coercion of Hell, Last Testament and the Sigils of the Art.* Enodia, 2019.

Brade, Anna-Elisabeth. "Efterskrift." In *Henrik Smiths Lægebog I-VI.* Copenhagen, 1976.

Cavallius, Gunnar Hyltén. *Wärend och wirdarne: ett försök i svensk etnologi,* Vol. 1. Stockholm, 1863.

Craigie, W. A. "Evald Tang Kristensen, a Danish Folk-Lorist." *Folklore,* Vol. 9, No. 3 (1898): 194-225.

Gårdbäck, Johannes Björn. "Cyprianus Förmaning" and "Cyprian Books of Magic in the Scandinavian Tradition." In *Cypriana: Old World,* eds. Alexander Cummins, Jesse Hathaway Diaz and Jenn Zahrt, 36-82. Revelore, 2016.

Gårdbäck, Johannes Björn. *Trolldom: Spells and Methods of the Norse Folk Magic Tradition.* YIPPIE, 2015.

Johnson, Thomas. *Svartkonsböcker.* Revelore, 2019.

Kotva, Simone. *Cyprianic Conjurations from Norway.* Hadean, 2024.

Leitão, José. *The Immaterial Book of St. Cyprian: Folk Concepts & Views on* The Book *as a Cultural Item Through the Reading of Folk Narratives.* Revelore, 2017.

Leitão, José. Trans. *The Book of St. Cyprian: The Sorcerer's Treasure.* Hadean, 2014.

Ohrt, Ferdinand. "Cyprianus: Hans Bog og hans Bøn." *Danske studier* (1923): 1-21.

Ohrt, Ferdinand. *Danmarks trylleformler,* 2 Vols. Copenhagen and Oslo, 1917-1921.

Ohrvik, Ane. *Medicine, Magic and Art in Early Modern Norway: Conceptualizing Knowledge.* Palgrave Macmillan, 2018.

Oja, Linda. *Varken Gud eller natur: synen på magi i 1600- och 1700-talets Sverige.* Stockholm, 1999.

Stokker, Kathleen. *Remedies and Rituals: Folk Medicine in Norway and the New Land.* Minnesota Historical Society Press, 2007.

Stokker, Kathleen. "Narratives of Magic and Healing: 'Oldtidens Sortebog' in Norway and the New Land," *Scandinavian Studies*, vol. 73, no. 3 (2001): 399–416.

Stokker, Kathleen. "Between Sin and Salvation: The Human Condition in Legends of the Black Book Minister." *Scandinavian Studies*, vol. 67, no. 1 (1995): 91–108.

Stokker, Kathleen. "To Catch a Thief: Binding and Loosing and the Black Book Minister." *Scandinavian Studies*, vol. 61, no. 4 (1989): 353–74.

Zahn, Theodor von. *Cyprian von Antiochien und die deutsche Faustsage.* Erlangen, 1892.

Index

.

www.ingramcontent.com/pod-product-compliance
Lightning Source LLC
Chambersburg PA
CBHW051434270326
41935CB00018B/1821

9 7 8 1 9 1 5 9 3 3 7 4 4